David Nelson Beach

The Newer Religious Thinking

David Nelson Beach

The Newer Religious Thinking

ISBN/EAN: 9783337262655

Printed in Europe, USA, Canada, Australia, Japan

Cover: Foto ©Lupo / pixelio.de

More available books at **www.hansebooks.com**

THE NEWER RELIGIOUS THINKING.

The words that I have spoken unto you are spirit, and are life.

I came that they may have life, and may have it abundantly.

THE LORD JESUS.

BY

DAVID NELSON BEACH.

BOSTON:
LITTLE, BROWN, AND COMPANY.
1893.

University Press:
JOHN WILSON AND SON, CAMBRIDGE, U.S.A.

TO THE MEMORY

OF

PRESTON SHELDON, M.D.

1854–1891.

---

*"Perplext in faith, but pure in deeds,
At last he beat his music out."*

Old things are passed away.
All things are become new.
All things are of God.
SAINT PAUL.

PREFACE.

THE newer religious thinking here spoken of is not mine, nor any other man's, nor that of any institution, or school, or division of Christendom. It is a world movement. It is the lineal descendant of world movements older than Abraham. I have not attempted to define it except in the most general way, nor to compass it, but only to speak sympathetically and suggestively of it.

I have not spoken technically, but in plain language. This is not a monograph. It is not specialist work. It is a talk about matters in everybody's thought. If I should characterize it at all, I should call it an interpretation, a trying to put new things and feared things — "they feared as they entered into the cloud" — in their simple and divine light.

Such touching evidences of its oral helpfulness have reached me that I commit it to type. In so far as God's mind is in it, may it reach men's minds. For there is sore need of light. And there is need that the light have in it warmth and vision. If even a little of this is here, may it gladden eyes and stir hearts.

Cambridge, Massachusetts,
April 29, 1893.

CONTENTS.

		PAGE
I.	THIS THINKING CHARACTERIZED	13
II.	ITS HUNGER AFTER GOD	39
III.	ITS PASSION FOR MEN	71
IV.	ITS THOUGHT OF NATURE, HISTORY, LIFE	101
V.	ITS IDEA OF THE BIBLE	131
VI.	CHRIST ITS CENTRE	161

APPENDICES.

A.	ONE TYPE OF NATURE TEACHING	189
B.	OMITTED PART OF DISCOURSE VI.	199
C.	SOME PLAIN QUESTIONING	213
	LIST OF PRINCIPAL NOTES	229

God is love.
In him is no darkness at all.
It doth not yet appear what we shall be.
We shall be like him.
SAINT JOHN.

THIS THINKING CHARACTERIZED.

SYNOPSIS.

Men are under a divine impulse. — It is from without, and yet from within. — This is what religion is. — Being thus life, it is ever renewing itself. — There always has been a newer religious thinking: In the Old Testament; In the New; Throughout the Christian ages; Now (examples). — This implies no instability in the facts of religion, but only an ever-enlarging apprehension of them. — The latter is ground for unspeakable joy. — Interesting fields of study opened by this fact. — What business have we to go heresy-hunting? — Certain indications of newer religious thinking at the present time: (1) Among men of unfaith; (2) Among "Unevangelicals;" (3) In the Church of Rome; (4) Among "Evangelicals." — Certain characteristics of this thinking: (1) Its scientific temper; (2) Its practical bent; (3) Its purpose to include in its concept the entire religious impulse of the world; (4) Its obedience unto the heavenly vision. — Something of eternity already shines in its face.

THE NEWER RELIGIOUS THINKING.

I.

THIS THINKING CHARACTERIZED.[1]

Wherefore, O king Agrippa, I was not disobedient unto the heavenly vision. — ACTS xxvi. 19.

A DIVINE compulsion is here acknowledged. It becomes the law of a great, aspiring, epoch-affecting life. And the compulsion, the law, are of the sort which alone can be most potent over human life. They spring from vision, from an illumination of the inner nature. They are thus a part of the man. They are from without him, and yet from within him. They demand great

[1] Preached at Prospect Street Church, Cambridge, Massachusetts, Sunday night, October 30, 1892. Somewhat amended here, but the *spoken form* retained. So of the later discourses.

thoughts, feelings, revisions, renovations. Slowly, perhaps reluctantly, they command his assent. But being of him as well as from beyond him, they move and transform him. They are life. In the obeying of them there is life. The living spirit cannot be disobedient to them.

This is what religion is. It is a something from outside, and yet from inside. It is the life of a man, of men, of peoples, of epochs; a part of them, and yet not of them so much as a reciprocity between them and their correlative in the nature of things, in the heart of the world, — in, for short, God. Being thus life, it is always renewing itself. It is ever young. There is always a newer religious thinking.

There always has been such thinking in the past. Noah is farther on than Enoch; Israel than Abraham; the Moses of Deuteronomy than the Moses of Exodus; Samuel than Joshua; David than Samuel, with that great discovery of his, " Thou desirest not sacrifice," and with that new face on nature, life, and religion, which ever in him appears. Isaiah is farther on, too, than Elijah; and the late Isaiah than the earlier. The Christ of the Peræan ministry is an advance over the Christ of the Galilean ministry.[1] Saint Peter at Cæsarea, ten years after Pentecost, confesses that God has made clear to him a truth until then unperceived, — a truth around the question of the correctness of which the apostolic history thenceforth turns. The Saint Paul of First and Second Timothy is farther on, not only by a decade, but in his intellectual outlook, than the

[1] Whether or not the Evangelists indicate an advance in the thinking of the Saviour during his public ministry, corresponding with his advance in method, is a question of interpretation; and since their testimony is indirect, the interpretation will be colored by one's insight and conception of developing character. It will also be colored, perhaps, by one's view of the person of Christ. My own view of his person is very high. Nevertheless, as his method advanced, so, it seems to me, did his mental outlook. Neither am I able to see why its earlier advance (Luke ii. 52) should have been stayed when he reached the period of intense activity which would most have furthered such advance. And since there is no finer test of character than its behavior under access of fresh light, particularly when one is amidst life, I should be sorry to think of the Saviour as not knowing the fellowship with us of such character-testing. "It behoved him in all things to be made like unto his brethren" (Heb. ii. 17).

Saint Paul of First and Second Corinthians. The Saint John of the Epistles sweeps a wider horizon than the Saint John at the Beautiful Gate of the Temple. On the open vision of the Greek Fathers succeeds the dogmatic rigidity of the Latin Fathers. Anselm treads broader fields than Gregory the Great. Luther, Zwingle, Calvin, exploit new fields, and dissentiently. Jonathan Edwards leads a new movement in the religious thought of New England, as well as that revival of its religious life known as the "Great Awakening." The history, in short, of the Old Testament and of the New, that which gave significance and permanence to the writings there gathered, is progress, clearer and yet clearer apprehensions of truth. The history, too, of the Christian Church, as Professor Allen, of our city, has so admirably outlined in his book, "The Continuity of Christian Thought," is a history of the unfolding of Christian ideas. As I said, there always has been a newer religious thinking. Those ages which seem to have been motionless, and their thought dormant, were moving. There was many a morning star of the Reformation in the Middle-Age night.

And as there always has been a newer religious thinking, so there is to-day. A book has been shown me, which belonged to the late Rev. Asa Bullard. It is marked, "To be preserved, as it is my only copy." It is without titlepage. It is Horace Bushnell's "Christian Nurture." It never got far enough in the hands of the Massachusetts Sabbath School Society, of which Mr. Bullard was the executive, — now our Congregational Sunday School and Publishing Society, — to have a titlepage or an imprint. Why? Because certain men who saw its advance sheets pronounced it heresy, and raised such an alarm about it that it was suppressed. That book, issued by other publishers, is now a classic. Nobody is afraid of it. Mr. Bullard rejoiced in it, as, for aught I know, he did from the start.[1]

---

[1] Mr. Bullard died April 5, 1888, aged eighty-four years and ten days. He had been a member of Prospect Street Church since 1857. A window to his memory was put into the church at Easter, 1892. Its subject is, "Christ Blessing Little Children," after Hofmann. It is inscribed: "In

When Professor Park was transferred from the chair of Homiletics to that of Theology at Andover, he was considered by many a very dangerous man. Controversy regarding his teachings waxed hot. Pamphlets, reviews, newspapers, assailed him. Now he is regarded as a bulwark of orthodoxy. When Prof. Nathaniel W. Taylor was teaching at New Haven, sixty years ago, matters now of commonest acceptance, Connecticut was convulsed to its centre with religious alarm against him, and the Seminary at East Windsor, now Hartford Seminary, was established to save the faith from his ravages. An elderly Englishman has recently contributed to one of our reviews, from personal recollection, the story of three religious panics in Great Britain, of a similar type, about matters that have ceased to give men anxiety. But let me summon you yourselves as witnesses.

Loving Memory of the Children's Minister, Rev. Asa Bullard: Born, 1804: Died, 1888: From Prospect Street Church and Sabbath School." Mr. Bullard did not agree in all respects theologically either with Dr. Bushnell or with the writer. The allusion here is only to his attitude toward Dr. Bushnell's book on the Christian upbringing of children.

Probably all of you whose lives have covered as many as twenty-five or thirty years have, consciously or unconsciously, somewhat changed your thought on religious matters. If you have not, I condole with you. Twenty-five or thirty years in such a world as this ought somewhat to modify the ablest thinking even on religious subjects.

Now what does this mean? Does it imply that the facts at the basis of religion are not trustworthy? Does it insinuate that everything in religion is relative, and a mere matter of point of view? Not at all. Such inferences were as absurd as to have inferred, when men were gradually accepting the Copernican astronomy, or modern geology, that sun and stars and earth were not trustworthy, and were only relative, and matters of point of view. Sun, stars, earth, in common with the facts at the basis of religion, change not. But man's measure of them, grasp of them, knowledge of them, and impressibleness by them, change with the growing mind and heart of man.

So far is such a state of things as I have

been describing from being ground for alarm, that it is ground, the rather, for devout and unspeakable joy. As Kepler cried out, on discovering the clew to the computation of the orbits of the heavenly bodies, "I think God's thoughts after him!" so does Saint Paul speak of the mystery hid through the ages, but now made known, and affirm that the chiefest of the apostles only sees as yet "in a mirror, darkly," but shall see "face to face." Every man, by reason of such a state of the case, becomes a discoverer of truths divine, and a medium through whom others may receive the knowledge of such truths; and the way is thus left open for an infinite progress in knowing, appreciating, and using the facts of religion. Any other state of the case would make future history a blank, and eternity a horror. For the world to go on, with progress in the apprehension of religious truth at an end,— seeing that religious truth is the deepest, the sweetest, the most transforming, — and for men, out of this world's toil, sweat, travail, weariness, and defeat, to be hurried on into an eternity in which our earth thoughts and earth measures of God were a finality, would be a fate of history and of humanity too fearful to contemplate. But such is not the fate, as these phenomena, from the earliest Hebrew history until this hour, abundantly and gloriously prove.

It would be interesting to make even a cursory study of the progress of religious thought in the Old Testament; of the same progress during the perhaps four centuries between Malachi and Christ; and of the same in the New Testament. This is a distinctively modern study, and is yet in its infancy. Toward it the new chairs of Biblical Theology, in various institutions, are contributing. With it, for comprehensiveness and balance, the study of other, and especially of contemporaneous religions, needs to go, — " comparative religions," as that study is often called. The same sort of study, similarly paralleled, for the Christian ages, would also be of great interest.

Fresher, because more recent, accessible,

and in touch with current thinking, would be a study of this progress during the present century, and particularly in Great Britain; because the study of that portion of it would include a relatively compact territory, history, and group of men. For this last, as I referred to Professor Allen's "Continuity of Christian Thought," in reference to the Christian ages, let me commend Tulloch's "Movements of Religious Thought in Britain during the Nineteenth Century." In these movements, the poets, of some of whom we have been thinking together recently, have had a far greater hand than Professor Tulloch indicates,—he having in that book treated only of distinctively religious writers. Tennyson's "In Memoriam," for example, marks a great "divide" and new upland in our century's outlook toward immortality. That service to human thinking would have been, of itself, an immeasurable gift to the world, had the Laureate written nothing else.

We cannot, however, go into these matters now. But there is a practical question we can go into. The question is this: What business have we to mutiny against this law of our being, the law of the Bible, the law of religious history, the law which hinders the future from being a blank and eternity a horror, and go heresy-hunting? They stoned heretics in the Old Testament. They cut off their heads and crucified them in the New. They invented the horrors of the Inquisition for them in the sixteenth century. We build the sepulchres of those heretics. We are always quoting them and praising them. We know that they discovered truth for us, and made the world better for us. Why, then, do we start off to be the ruin of heretics now? Why do we hold the clothes of them that stone them? Have we not a measure of common-sense? Do we care to repeat the folly of trying to suppress the Horace Bushnells, the Nathaniel W. Taylors, the Professor Parks, of nowadays? Surely we shall be laughed at some day for doing this. Perhaps we shall live long enough to laugh at ourselves. Mr. Bullard, with his sense of humor, must have edged off into a smile and then into a laugh, when he saw that poor thin little Bushnell book, without any titlepage or imprint, and with its "To be preserved, as it is my only copy." There were soon copies enough.

Turning, however, from these reflections, let us notice, first, certain indications, and then certain characteristics, of the newer religious thinking at the present time.

I. Certain indications.

1. And, to begin with, even unbelief, in its truer, more typical phases, is in a hopeful state of newness and progress. It does not scoff; it is sorry not to believe. Its quarrel is with extreme partisans of faith, not with those humble, teachable souls who live their faith. Witness divisions XXXI., XXXII., and XXXIII., of "In Memoriam" as an expression, indeed from a somewhat different point of view, of this new attitude.

2. Those Christians, moreover, commonly termed "unevangelical" are likewise in a certain refreshing newness and progress of thought. Those of them often called "radicals," while moving away from some of the

simpler facts of religion, are in many instances taking the most commendable steps toward the practical aspects of the religious life; while the so-called "moderates" are adopting thoughts and methods which bring them nearer to the so-called "evangelical" religionists. They hunger for a warmer, more pronounced religious experience; for meetings for prayer; for mission work; for such work even among the heathen; and for some ground of unity which may bring them into closer touch with the Church universal.

This might be abundantly illustrated were there time. The *odium theologicum*, if not passed, is passing. And as a liberal spirit among so-called "Evangelicals" is often the cause of much reproach to its possessors, so among the classes already referred to, those who are moving in this newness and progress are often maligned for doing so. The superintendent of the non-sectarian East End Christian Union, of our city, tells of meeting a Trinitarian who did not want to contribute toward it because it was too liberal, and then a Unitarian who found fault with it because it was too orthodox. And with the thought underlying the superintendent's plain rejoinder, " I told both of them that I had no use for such men," the truer spirits of both wings will tend more and more to agree.

3. Think, again, how in the Church of Rome there are also the progressives; how the present Pope is in this respect an advance on the last; how men like the revered pastor of one of our Cambridge Catholic churches, while no less Catholics, are pushing forward — often at the expense of that obloquy from their associates which the prophets and apostles of progress have generally to encounter — into a practical fellowship with religious men outside their ancient communion.

4. Once more, in the religious bodies nearer ourselves than any of these, reflect, for example, on the coming of the Episcopal Church toward Phillips Brooks; on the tightening fellowship of the Presbyterian Church, which revolts from schism in the

case of Union Seminary and of Professor Briggs, whom such organs of conservatism as the "New York Observer" have long been scourging outrageously; and on the disposition of our own denomination to include rather than to expel men, churches, and institutions of learning, on which a section of the religious press has waged war for years.[1]

In the light of facts like these, it may be unhesitatingly affirmed that there is a greater unity amidst diversity, a greater respect for differences of opinion, a greater bringing of all questions to the test of life and of spirit, and a larger, truer thinking about God, and

---

[1] On the primary movement now going on in human nature toward inclusiveness and solidarity, see Professor Tucker's memorable Phi Beta Kappa Oration at Harvard, June 30, 1892. These sentences in it bear on that portion of the subject here alluded to: —

"Questions are arising in our time, and passing into heated discussion, of the most fundamental and vital kind, which in other times would have split the most compact body, but thus far they have not divided a single communion. The one ecclesiastical sin of our age is schism. Of that alone we are intolerant" (pp. 18, 19).

The Oration is entitled, "The New Movement in Humanity from Liberty to Unity." Houghton, Mifflin, and Company, Boston. 1892.

life, and truth, to-day, among religious people the likest to ourselves, than there has ever been before; and that we, in this respect, are, as I have intimated, wittingly or unwittingly, in the current of a great world-movement in similar directions, embracing "Unevangelicals" as well as "Evangelicals," Catholics as well as Protestants, and the truer types of unbelievers as well as believers. Thus is the prayer, "Thy kingdom come," getting its answer, — slowly, with many a reverse, with sore travail still, but surely. He whose right it is already reigns, and is marshalling events, movements, men, opinions, into compacter, truer lines of tendency, expectation, and promise; all of which shall eventuate according to that "heavenly vision" which, whether we will or not, we cannot choose but obey, and the ending whereof the wisest and the most far-sighted only sees as "in a mirror, darkly."

II. Next, and in conclusion, let us try to fix in our minds certain characteristics of the newer religious thinking of our time.

1. One of them is its scientific temper.

The thinking of which I speak is not going on in this century of the vastest expansion of the boundaries of knowledge that the world has ever known without being affected at once by the knowledge, and by those processes of induction and of deduction by which the knowledge has come. It grows tired of theories. It wants facts. After these it is groping everywhere, — in the world of nature, in the field of archæology, in that mighty research for a true account of the origin of the human species, often caricatured as a trying to prove one's descent from apes, but a far deeper and wider reaching investigation than the caricaturists dream; in heredity, too, in animal psychology, in sociology, in the history of opinions, and in those seers, the prophets, psalmists, and poets of all time.

It wants the truth, nothing but the truth, and will have it at all hazards; and is unalterably purposed to count nothing finally settled, until it matches in with God's whole book of nature as well as of grace, and of the human heart as well as of metaphysics.

And since there is no schism in the truth, but truth agrees with itself, verifies itself, and is a unity, we ought to be devoutly thankful that such a purpose marks the newer religious thinking.

2. Another characteristic of this thinking is its practical bent.

"What can religion do for a man?" it seems forever to be asking. That which, more than anything else, has sickened it of over-confidence in certain systematic ways of looking at truth is the miserable fruit of such systems. It does not want a religion professing to follow the forgiving Jesus, if that religion does not make men forgiving. It does not want a religion of love which does not make men loving. It does not want a religion which teaches that all men are brothers, if it produces the class distinctions, the outrageous disparities between wealth and poverty, and that luxurious selfishness so common, hardly less in the Church than out of it, in our time.

Furthermore, when it accepts religion, albeit never so devotedly, it is not content with prayers, sacraments, sound doctrine, and religious routine. In these it believes. But it wants something adequate to show for them in deeds. It is willing to invest heavily in religion, but demands dividends in bettered lives, ennobled communities, and truer political, economic, intellectual, and social conditions.

3. Yet another characteristic of the newer religious thinking is its purpose to include in its concept the entire religious impulse of the world.

When "they therefore that were scattered abroad upon the tribulation that arose about Stephen travelled" far, "speaking the word to none save only to Jews," until an almost accidental experiment taught them better, they did what religion has characteristically done until our time. That God was with and in the religious life of the Egyptians, Assyrians, Greeks, Romans, etc., as well as with and in the religious life of the Hebrews, has been little recognized until recently. But he was. No race, no people, no history, has a monopoly of religion. Religion is a great fact. It is a part of the race of man. It is the correlation of man and what is above and beyond him.

The newer religious thinking recognizes this comprehensiveness. It is trying to understand all religions. It hopes, through the religions and religious impulses of all peoples, to bring in the simpler, clearer, and final religion. Hence the men of faith are reaching out and striking hands with the men who, until recently, would have been called the men not of faith, to help them and to receive help. To illustrate what I mean: Almost no man ever helped me more in spiritual things — I say, please note, "helped me," not I him — than a friend of mine, now passed on into the infinite light, who was to such an extent an agnostic that, for a long time, he could not so much as pray. But his life was a faith, a prayer, a holiness, such that he was a new manifestation of God to my life, and to the lives of all who knew him.[1] In such a sense as this, the men of faith are striking hands with men hitherto

[1] It is to his memory that this book is inscribed.

generally counted not of faith, for mutual help.

Similarly the newer religious thinking despairs not that the different divisions of Christendom, heretofore seemingly hopelessly estranged, and all theistic religions, and indeed all religions, have contributions to make toward, and in some sense a place to take in, the ampler and more adequate religious life that is to be. This is the same thing as to say, not only that the newer religious thinking has a scientific temper, but that it has at length come to recognize religion in its every form as a great, scientific, and mightily instructive fact. Please observe that, in making this statement, I have no time to define and clarify it. Because I do not do so, it may be that I shall be misunderstood. But when "men of every tribe, and tongue, and people, and nation" are represented as contributing to the apocalyptic glory, it is impossible for me to believe that the religions, and religious capacities, receptivities, and aptitudes of "every tribe, and tongue, and people, and nation" are not also taken into the account, and given their range and use. "God," we read, "is no respecter of persons;" and I beg leave to doubt if, any more, he is a respecter of religions.

4. Finally, while the newer religious thinking is scientific in temper, practical in bent, and is enlarging its concept of religion, let no man say, or even imagine, that this thinking is other than inspired by, and obedient unto, a "heavenly vision," which ever hovers in its foreground, and beckons it on.

The boundaries of its belief may be lessened, for it doubts much; but the depths and heights of that belief are infinite. Out on a simple, real, honest confidence it ventures, like Abraham scarce knowing whither it goes, but sure that it must leave not only Ur of the Chaldees, but Haran, and come into a place which it is after to receive for an inheritance.

God, for it, is no longer in a creed, however true the creed may be; nor in any book, however priceless; nor in any organization, however venerable and sacred; nor in any form or observance, however helpful in itself; nor here, nor there, nor accessible in thus and such a manner; but God is with the man, — in him, about him, beyond him, his Father, Helper, Friend, and All-sufficiency.

And he himself is in God's universe, nor ever can get out of it; so that even mysterious heaven grows simple, being God's; and he does not crave so much to be in heaven, even, as to be in such a mind as God is in, and as to be helping some other God's-child, his brother, though he were fathoming hell to find him.

And for him fear is done; for has not perfect love cast it out? And hope is ever fresh; for can he ever wholly find out God, or sound God's love's-depth? And as for motive, of the want or badness whereof so many complain, that is no longer his solicitude; for has not the same marched on him, seized him, and possessed itself of him forever, even the movement of none other than the living God motive henceforth in him? True, he expects nothing other than to descend again and again into the depths, — cast down many a time, defeated, spent; but went there not One before him thither? Shall he not follow so kingly a Forerunner? And has not all this a purpose?

But, truth to tell, he is reluctant so much as to think of himself. Self, in fact, is getting out of him. Truth, reality, God, are getting in. Herein, too, he is "not disobedient unto the heavenly vision," and therefore wots not that that vision is even now transfiguring him, and that something of eternity already shines in his face.

ITS HUNGER AFTER GOD.

SYNOPSIS.

Hunger after God the propulsion of newer religious thinking. — Jacob and Moses illustrate this. — Why it is necessarily so. — The receivers and revelators of larger religious truth have become such by reason of their hunger for it (examples). — Sketch of the upgrowth of the newer religious thinking of our time. — The newer literature contained it, in principle, but religious thinkers were specially its channel. — Coleridge and Bushnell; their wide influence. — The Tractarians. — Necessarily, over against the two tendencies represented by the foregoing, came Arnold, Robertson, Maurice, Kingsley, etc. — Their application of religion to life. — The Germanic contribution; contrast between it and the Anglo-Saxon. — The thinking of this decade an advance on that outlined above, by reason of ampler data through long inductive work. — America, until recently, provincial in this matter. — The sketch suggests how hunger after God has impelled the movement. — Personal testimony. — This hunger necessitates image-breaking in theology. — Mr. Beecher's remarks in connection with his "Background of Mystery." — Some idols needing overthrow: (1) The machine thought of God; there is a Biblical pantheism; (2) Exaggeration of the idea of God as ruler; God not mainly that; (3) Undue insistence on the philosophy of the Trinity; how far that doctrine may rightly go; (4) God in Christ as mainly governmental or forensic; the facts can never be included under this category; Christ a vital, living, present Saviour. — Other idols suggested. — The Good Tidings unspeakably hurt by such misrepresentations of God. — The Church, the clergy, the laity, in fact all true souls, have herein a heavy responsibility laid on them.

II.

ITS HUNGER AFTER GOD.[1]

And Jacob asked him, and said, Tell me, I pray thee, thy name. — GENESIS xxxii. 29.
And Moses said unto God, Behold, when I come unto the children of Israel, and shall say unto them, The God of your fathers hath sent me unto you; and they shall say to me, What is his name? what shall I say unto them? — EXODUS iii. 13.
And he said, Show me, I pray thee, thy glory. — EXODUS xxxiii. 18.

THE newer religious thinking of the present proves its kinship to the newer religious thinking of all time in finding its propulsion in a profound hunger after God.

Jacob, who wished to know the name of his mysterious visitor, and Moses, who put the same question, and desired to behold God's glory, epitomize the natural history of all truly unfolding religious thought. Here is the man; somewhere, in him, be-

[1] Prospect Street, Sunday night, November 6, 1892.

yond him, is infinite reality, — in one word, God. Religion is that verity, partly conceptual, partly factual, which correlates the two. And because life is life, because the living man thinks, feels, and grows, his thought of this verity, his conception of religion, grows. But the object of his conception, namely, religion, being a correlation, being a something from within him as well as from beyond him, he is not passive in his growing religious thought. He is active; he thinks; he feels. He strives to clarify his thinking and feeling; he hungers after knowledge of the infinite; he yearns toward God. "Tell me, I pray thee, thy name," he cries; "Show me, I pray thee, thy glory." And the hunger, the cry, the attitude of interest and inquiry before that bush, burning but not consumed, which the universe is, and the struggle, as of one wrestling in the night, with the mysterious problems of life and of destiny, predispose a man to receive impressions, light, and new religious life. "He that seeketh, findeth."

It is not, therefore, by accident or partiality that the wrestling Jacobs, and the inquiring and seeking men like Moses, receive, each in his fashion, new thoughts, ideals, and principles in the range of religion. Indeed, it might be summarily said, without fear of successful contradiction, that the receivers and revelators of larger truth, particularly in the realm of religion, — whether they have been such receivers and revelators publicly or privately, in a widely recognized manner or not, or within the bounds of one form of religion or of another, — have become the channels for receiving and revealing such larger truth, through their own hunger for it, their own impressibleness by it, and their own receptivity and responsiveness to it.

Thus all the newer religious thinking, worthy the name, whether in the past or in the present, has had its spring in hunger after God. Jacob and Moses, Samuel and David, Elijah and Isaiah, Saint Paul and Saint John, Origen and Augustine, Gregory the Great and Anselm, Luther and Knox, John Bunyan and Jonathan Edwards, John Wesley and John Henry Newman, Maurice and Bushnell, Phillips Brooks and Father Hall, — these, in common with the lowliest waiters on truth divine, have received and given out the divine impulse, as hungering for it, seeking it, filled with it, transformed by it, and as thereby the mediums through which it has passed into the possession of mankind. What a lesson is there not for us here, to be open, receptive, hungering toward God, and, as freely receiving, so to be freely giving! For of this truly sacramental privilege, as of that other spoken of by Lowell, it remains true that —

> "The Holy Supper is kept, indeed,
> In whatso we share with another's need;
> Not what we give, but what we share, —
> For the gift without the giver is bare."

But, to be more specific: —

I. Let us, in the first place, bring rapidly before our minds a little of the way in which this century's newer religious thinking has come down to us; and let us be asking ourselves meanwhile whether, looked at as regards the men identified with it, this thinking is not akin, as I observed at the outset, to the newer religious thinking of all time, in finding its propulsion in a profound hunger after God.

This thinking, with its corresponding hunger, then, let us not forget, was already abroad, in less definite manifestation, in the newer literature which ushered in this century, — in Burns, for example, and Coleridge, and Wordsworth, yes, even in Shelley. It was caught up and developed in our epoch-marking poets, in Tennyson, in Lowell, in Browning.

But in men approaching with an especially religious wistfulness the burning bush of the universe, the Peniel of human existence, it most strongly appeared. Coleridge, now thought of as religious thinker rather than as poet, made a way for it in England; Bushnell, in America.[1] It is difficult for us of the immediate present to understand how

---

[1] No study of the history of this subject, in America, should omit the relation to it of Dr. Channing, Theodore Parker, and Ralph Waldo Emerson. Nor, on both sides of the Atlantic, should the impulse toward earnestness, reality, and moral enthusiasm which was afforded by Thomas Carlyle be overlooked.

vast was the influence which Coleridge exerted on the religious thinkers of the generation now aging and aged on both sides the Atlantic. One of that generation, a leader of that branch of the Christian Church of which he was a clergyman, and now long passed on into eternal light, told me, in the first year of my ministry, that Coleridge was as real a personality to him as if he had been his companion and intimate friend. He had entered as living power into that man's life. Bushnell had a like influence. He was read abroad with hardly less interest than in America. He was particularly powerful in the pulpit. His prayers were as if he stood in the presence-chamber, not only of infinite majesty, but of infinite truth and clearness of vision and power of illumination. In advanced age, in the chapel of Yale College, preaching as I never heard other mortal preach, he first gave me — in crude beginnings — some grasp on things eternal. Both men were John the Baptists, forerunners of our new temper in religion. They were dwelling ever on the spirit and meaning of nature, of events, of mind, and of life. They were tracing the analogies of things natural and things spiritual. The title of one of Bushnell's books, " Nature and the Supernatural," typifies both men.

But between the men of Coleridge's temper and the literal religionists of England, there sprang antagonisms; and amidst the uncertainties and contentions consequent thereupon, and due also to other causes which were likewise at work, there started a type of newer thinking which concentrated attention on institutional Christianity, on the Church, on its traditions, usages, and authority. This was the Tractarian movement. Some men in it, like Newman, went to Rome; some, like Pusey, into the high-church side of Protestantism. Mightily stimulating to thought, study, and the personal religious life, were these men. They, too, were helpful builders of the spiritual temple.

In such a state of affairs, because men in religion could neither be mainly idealists, as Coleridge was, nor mainly Churchmen as the

Tractarians were, but must be in life, and hold a living faith that could shape England's politics and help England's poor, that could recover a foothold of trust again for men far gone toward unbelief, and could satisfy minds as penetrating as Tennyson's and Browning's,— there began to come forward men hard to classify, so new, fresh, strong, were their utterances and their thoughts: Thomas Arnold, Frederick W. Robertson, Frederick Denison Maurice, Charles Kingsley, and many others of a like temper on both sides of the Atlantic, though few indeed comparable to these.

It was the magnificent service of such men that they recovered for religion its hold on life: Arnold, for example, on the men of Rugby and of the universities; Robertson on such a populous and frivolous watering-place as Brighton; Maurice on the students of Lincoln's Inn, and on the London workingmen; and Kingsley on town and country living, on scientific pursuits, and on the burning questions of a practical nature which were agitating England. It was their magnificent service, likewise, to show that doubt may be the doorway of faith; that reason has its place in religion, indeed that religion is the highest reason; that, moreover, beyond formal reason there is a reason intuitional, of insight, of vision, and of the living "Word" of God in men's souls; and above all, that Christianity is a present, living, and constructive force in society and in the life of individuals, in distinction from being a tradition, an observance, or a pious piece of partialism.

Other lands, other faiths, and indeed, as I suggested in the last discourse, unfaiths, had their parts to contribute to the newer religious thinking. On them I cannot dwell otherwise than to testify how greatly the Teutonic mind, in point of research, of systematizing, and of insight, has stimulated scholarship, has accumulated intellectual material, and has moved philosophically toward the spirit and unity of all religions. To this mind, to the land and race of Luther, the newer religious thinking owes measureless obligations. Nevertheless, for religion in application, for it in its relations to the nation, to society, to home, and to the heart, — for, in short, religion in its more concrete aspects, — Germany has not in my judgment, done for the world that peculiar living service which has characterized in particular the constructive minds of Great Britain, and, to a less degree, of their kin this side the sea.

We of this decade belong in a distinctly different stage of the newer religious thinking from that to which Robertson, Maurice, and their group belonged. We have a vast accumulation of facts now well ascertained, which was not within the reach of those men, and which was, as it were, only divined by them from afar. We have in general a far richer archæology than they; in particular, a more adequate grasp of remote history, and of the processes at work in prehistoric times; a wider acquaintance with religions and with race tendencies; great gains in critical knowledge of how the Bible came to be, and of Hebrew history; and, comprehensively, an exacter science alike in regard to the forces at work in nature, in society, and in human life. All these, with their inevitable modification and enrichment of a thinking much cruder then than now, have brought the men of the present to positions and tendencies in thought which were not to have been expected then.

Indeed, when some sense of all this comes in on the mind like a flood, how can one repress a cry to God that we may not be dull and unwitting, but may understand our time, sympathize with it, appreciate its mighty meaning, get at least a little way into that meaning ourselves, and make it potent in ourselves and in all about us? But on the spirit of those men, on their splendid courage, on their insight into spiritual things, and on their unshaken resolve, come what might, that religion should lay hold on life, — on these elements in them we have not advanced, nor shall we in many a day.

It ought further to be remarked that we in America, having been engaged in building up this great country of ours, in fighting our war through, in grappling with the questions thence issuing, and withal, by our tariffs, our trusts, our speculations, and our shrewdnesses, in getting money faster than any other nation, and in spending it faster, have until recently stood aside somewhat provincially from the great, hard, thorough religious thinking beyond the seas; so that such gatherings as the general Congregational Council in London in 1891, where religious leaders of the same communion in America meet those of England and the Continent, bring forcibly to mind the fact that, theologically, many of us need to set our watches considerably ahead in order to tell Greenwich time.

Getting and spending money, if done in righteousness, and developing a great country such as ours, are good. One may, indeed, be permitted the inquiry whether they are the highest good, — whether a people may not be too rich, and whether a country may not, like a spindling child, develop faster than is for its permanent advantage. Certain at any rate it is that our brethren beyond the sea have surpassed us in the getting and practical expenditure of the riches of Godward and manward thinking, and in developing a country consisting, not of granite and of prairie loam, but of reasonableness, righteousness, and truth. To them we may well turn with teachable minds, — not necessarily to agree with them in all respects, but to emulate their noble studies and lofty thoughts.

In this rapid survey of the way along which the newer religious thinking of this century has travelled until it has reached us, I hope has appeared, at least impliedly, what I now affirm, that the persons, known or unknown, who have been most hospitable to it, and have most furthered it, have been moved, like Jacob or Moses, with great and earnest hungerings after God. His true, real, meaning-full name, his glory and himself, have been the objects of their quest. Not longer the Holy Grail, but very God, has allured them on.

No one who knew Arnold of Rugby, with whom religion was the heart of everything;

or Maurice, whose very face, manner, and bearing became a holy benediction, often remarked upon as he walked the streets; or Kingsley, for whom the whole world was, like his own Chester, God's wonderful cathedral, — no one, I say, who knew these men could well avoid likening them to typical men in Bible times. And as for Robertson, England has not seen, nor shall see, one hungering more for God. Such a temper, too, was in the Tractarian movement. Newman, as much as Robertson, sought God. A friend of mine who visited him toward the close of his life, could not give an account of the interview without conveying the most vivid impression of his saintliness. Such a temper, differently manifesting itself, animated Wordsworth, Tennyson, Browning. The Germans, in their prodigious labors for a better religious thinking, have, in their truer representatives, been devout too. So have our own people. So has many a man outside religious lines, and many a man seemingly outside of all faith.

It is right, on such a point as this, that

I should bear my personal testimony. If you have ever seen in me any unselfishness, any love of men, any grasp of affairs, any public spirit, any courage of conviction, any anything that is true, then let me say to you that the mightiest incentive thereto which I have ever known has been that vision of God, more simply and as I believe more truly conceived of, which in an ever-increasing degree commands me. It was so in the long ago of which I just now spoke, when God, through Horace Bushnell, awakened my soul. It was so seven years since, when, led as I believe of God, I unfolded to you my simpler conviction respecting our Lord's work.[1] It is so, if I know my own heart, as I speak to you in these discourses. And if I, who am so deficient, find God, more simply thought of, so much more to my life, and such a propulsion to truer thinking, how much more may we suppose this to be true of the veritable

---

[1] The two sermons, with some notes and additional matter, form the little book, "Plain Words on Our Lord's Work." Cupples, Upham, and Company, Boston. 1886.

leaders of religious thought, the holy prophets and seers of our time.

II. If now I have succeeded in making evident, by way of narrative and from individual illustrations, the fact to which I have also felt constrained to bear my personal testimony, namely, that hunger after God actuates the newer religious thinking, let me point out, in the second place, and as completing this discourse, some ways in which this hunger works practically.

Dr. Lyman Abbott, in the sermon preached in Plymouth Church the Sunday morning after Mr. Beecher's death, made this statement: "When your pastor preached that famous sermon on the 'Background of Mystery,' which created so much excitement and produced so much criticism, I went to him with the proofs of it. It was to be published in 'The Christian Union,' and I said to him: 'Mr. Beecher, this sermon you must revise.' I think it was the only time I ever had a controversy with Mr. Beecher and came out best, but he yielded that time. . . . And then I remember his turning to me, his great form growing greater, and the great brow growing higher, and his great eyes flashing fire, as he said something like this: 'There are times, in preaching, when I have a conception of the greatness and the goodness and the mercy and the love of my God, and then see by the side of it the hideous idols that are put up in Christian temples and represented in Christian literature, that are maligning my God; and I *hate* them, as the old Hebrew prophets hated the idols of old time, with an unutterable hatred; and'— then, with one of those sudden transitions, he dropped back and said — 'something's got to give way.'"

In this connection one remembers the zeal of the old image-breakers, say in Antwerp Cathedral in the time of William the Silent, or on many an occasion in the life of Israel. The image, or the idol, seemed such a travesty of God that the moral indignation almost passed bounds. But not all the idols are of wood, or of stone. Some of them are of the mind, — ideas, conceptions, doctrines. We worship sometimes the Bible more than the Holy Spirit, speaking within us as it spake to holy men of old. We worship sometimes our ideas of Christ's work more than we worship Christ. We worship sometimes human names and human authority more than we worship the living God.

Now the newer religious thinking, understanding by the light of history when it was that more or less of these images were set up (even as Christ did when he said, "Moses for your hardness of heart suffered you to" do a certain thing, " but from the beginning it hath not been so "), hungers to such a degree after God, and to have God no longer obscured and misrepresented by these images, that, like the old image or idol breakers, those to whom the clearer vision has come cannot but do what in them lies to break the idols down. Their course looks, to those not understanding it, like sacrilege. It seems inexplicable. But in reality it is hunger after God manifesting itself in this form.

May all such not feel "hate," except in Mr. Beecher's beneficent sense. May they

Its Hunger after God.

have, the rather, a loving and pitying spirit, although firm and thorough in their work. And when it costs them much, as many a time it will, may they have the spirit of the Lord Jesus, who broke down idol after idol of Jewish prejudice, but wept over Jerusalem, and prayed, "Father, forgive them," for those who avenged the broken idols by crucifying him.

What, let us ask, then, are some of the idols which the newer religious thinking, in this its hunger after God, would fain throw down?

1. One of them I may characterize as a machine or mechanical conception of God,— God as making the universe out of hand, like a machine; God as dwelling apart from the universe, as the makers of a gigantic ocean steamship, having built it, turn it off to ply back and forth without them on the stormy deep; and God as about to break up the universe, very much as if it were only so much junk.

Now, that there are expressions in the Bible regarding his forming the universe, doing what he wishes with it, and destroying it, admits of no question. But from these it cannot follow that such is an adequate representation of his relation to the universe. There are other and different expressions, which represent him as in his works, as delighting in them, as clothing himself with them. But the former type of representations, and the natural tendency of ages preceding this to look at matters mechanically, have brought it about that the ordinary conception of the relation of God to the universe is of the inadequate type which I have described.

This is a heavy reflection on God. It runs counter to our deepest instincts. It is contrary to reason that so vast, intricate, and mysterious a world, so athrill with thought and life, should be mechanical, a thing thrown off, a mere machine. It is contrary, also, to the teachings of science, which more and more are deepening the mystery of the universe. It is opposed, moreover, to the ruling expressions in the Bible. Not so do the minds which appear in the opening chapters of Genesis conceive of the world. His Spirit, as they suppose, broods it. He finds it very good. Men cannot get to the best of it, because they will not live truly enough, but God's angels can. Within it he himself walks in the cool of the day. So reverent of this earth are those far-off men! Not so, either, does Saint Paul conceive of the world. "The invisible things of him since the creation of the world are clearly seen, being perceived through the things that are made, even his everlasting power and divinity," exclaims the Apostle; and he represents the universe as sympathetically in a groaning and travail with the world-long birth of mental and spiritual life.

"But," says some one, "a thought of the universe contrary in this respect to the traditional one would issue in pantheism." Ah, my friend, you are at the usual tactics; employing deduction from imperfect conceptions, instead of induction from the fullest possible data, and sounding an unwarrantable alarm. Let us not be frightened at a name. Pantheism, by itself, is inadequate enough;

but there is a divine, yes a Biblical pantheism, — all things in God, by him, through him; all things standing together in him; he in his world, not apart from it; his world uttering him, expressing him, bodying him forth.

No epoch since Hebrew and Greek poets sang, except that period which has succeeded, though the least spiritual, in fastening upon us a large part of our religious ideas, namely, the Middle Ages, could have had the Bible in hand, and propounded in this respect a view of the universe utterly repugnant to the spirit of the Bible. This mechanical thought of God in his relation to the world must go; the more spiritual thought of him as immanent, as pervading the world, and as of it, though more than it, must come. The world is sacred. Existence is divine. There is nothing in which God is not. Ah! the beauty, the glory, the meaning, the comfort herefrom! How machine-like, with the lathe-marks still showing, is the counter graven image!

2. Another idol, or misrepresentation of God, is the conception of him as mainly ruler.

Its Hunger after God.

He rules, no doubt; but even in that there is nothing arbitrary, wilful, or absolute in temper. He rules by virtue of righteousness and of love. He is God because he is good. Moreover, the idea of him as ruler, when most correct, is only one of many aspects of him. And yet almost our whole theology is keyed to this idea,— his sovereignty, his laws, his jealousy for them, his punishments for those violating them, his wrath, his being unable to do this and that because he could not do it and be just, and very much more to the same effect.

Perhaps you know a great and noble man, a parent perchance, a magistrate, a college president like Mark Hopkins. He rules? Certainly. But is not his ruling the smallest aspect of him? Are you thinking, any great part of the time, that such a one is a ruler, — he being so much else, and so wonderfully so much else? So our Saviour has not much to say of God as ruler. He says something of that; but mainly he speaks of him as Father; as exercising a providential care over even the hairs of our heads; as yearning for the prodigal's return; as, like a true shepherd, having more joy of the lost sheep found than of the ninety and nine that went not astray. God, to the Saviour's thought, is one near us, with whom we may commune and become one, far more than a ruler.

This primary proposition, then, of mediæval theology, which has colored nearly every article of our creeds, must, I will not say go, for there is some truth in it, but must drop to its subordinate and normal place, and yield to other as the predominant aspects of God.

3. Still another idol, or misrepresentation of him, is one which I hesitate to mention, because my meaning may readily be misunderstood. But I cannot conscientiously avoid doing so. I refer to our philosophy of the Trinity, in so far as it is put in the place of God, — and it is put there a great deal, as I cannot help believing.

As a philosophy, although bunglingly expressing itself, it is in my judgment true. I believe, that is to say, in the reality and eternity of those distinctions in God's being which the terms Father, Son, and Holy Spirit answer to. I am, in short, philosophically a Trinitarian; and by this philosophy I most readily explain to myself those Biblical expressions, — so that, to this degree, I may add that I am Biblically a Trinitarian. Hegel's philosophy, unless I mistake, would, if it went so far, turn out to be Trinitarian. Much of the strongest thinking since Nicæa, early in the fourth century, has been Trinitarian. All this should weigh with a thoughtful person.

But one must distinguish between his theory or philosophy of certain facts, however venerable it may be, and the facts themselves. The facts are there. They cannot well be set aside. But our philosophy of the facts may be imperfect, or even mistaken. God, as Father, Son, and Holy Spirit, is in the Bible, and is to a large degree in human experience. That is fact. But our fourth-century and Hegelian philosophy of it is quite another thing. It may be correct, — I think it correct; but when I suppose that philosophy to compass God, and when I make representations accordingly, I attempt to measure him by the yardstick of Athanasius, or of Hegel, or of my own mind; and therein I am guilty, very possibly, of setting up an idol; and all idols must come down.

To the simple Biblical indications, and to those same indications in human experience, we cannot but adhere. But to a philosophy of them, which may or may not be correct, which certainly is extra-Biblical, and which has this ominous fact attending it, namely, that there have always been devout souls which could not accept it, — we may adhere personally, as I for one do; but we have no right authoritatively to impose it on others. We are, in other words, for liberty's sake, and for the truth's sake, to stop representing that God is necessarily expressed by our philosophy of the Trinity; but are, so far as we touch upon the subject, to represent that God is God, spoken of in the Bible as Father, Son, and Holy Spirit, and to a large degree so apprehended in human experience. This is Biblical, factual, and enough. What exceeds this verges toward image-making. It ought, moreover, — what is a burning shame, — no longer to separate Christian brethren.

4. One more idol, or misrepresentation of God, lies in our too frequent insistence that God in Christ is mainly governmental or forensic in his purpose.

Christ, according to this view, is almost entirely compassed by the idea that he became man, lived, suffered, and died, to get a law adjustment between sin, which God wished to forgive, and justice which prevented God from forgiving it.

This idol was set up in the eleventh century; for until that time the Church made Christ, the rather, to have been a negotiator with Satan for man's escape from hell. Since the eleventh century it has met with a variety of fortunes.

It is, indeed, a sort of corollary from the exaggerated emphasis laid in earlier ages on the idea of God as ruler. It gets some support from certain passages in the New Testament; just as the earlier idea of Christ as negotiating with Satan gets some support from certain other passages. But these passages are far from coextensive with the subject. There is a much wider range of Bible teaching. And the facts can never be included under this category. This its insufficiency was what compelled that investigation which led to my abandoning it, as intimated a few moments ago.

Christ is a vital, living, present Saviour; not a law expedient. The latter interpretation of him presupposes in God an attitude toward sin in his children for which, if you or I had the same toward sin in our children, we should loathe ourselves, or ought to. As you know, I depend wholly on Christ for salvation, that is, as the medium of spiritual life; but I should deny the truth as God gives me to see it if I explained his work forensically, and should, I am persuaded, be misrepresenting God likewise.

Against, thus, a machine or mechanical conception of God; against a conception of him which exaggerates his rulership out of all proportion to larger aspects of him;

against a conception which limits the thought of him to a philosophy, approximating the truth, as I personally believe, but which may or may not be correct, which is extra-Biblical, and which is incapable of being received by not a few devout minds; and against a conception of him which mainly interprets the glorious and life-affecting manifestation of himself in Christ by terms better suited to the law courts of the tyrannous Middle Ages, such as the "Merchant of Venice" brings before our minds, than to this age or to the facts,—against such conceptions of God, as misrepresentations of him, and as idols of the mind, the newer religious thinking utters its protest.

I might instance others. In particular, I should like to speak of our ordinary thought as not giving God time enough, nor scope enough, to come down to now, or to go on from now, or to include his whole great universe and his whole great family. But to do this to-night is impracticable. Besides, as examples, the idols already mentioned will suffice.

Let me say, in closing, that the "gospel of the glory of the blessed God" has been unspeakably hurt by such misrepresentations. Because it has been so misrepresented, multitudes have wandered off into unbelief. Other multitudes have groped blindly after God, with sick hearts. The enemies of Christianity have made the most of such caricatures, and have summarily bowed it out of court. These caricatures, and others like them, are the stock in trade of rank and noisy infidelity.

Brethren, the Church, the clergy, the laity, in fact all true souls, have herein a heavy responsibility laid on them. They are to think rightly of God, and speak rightly, and witness by true lives rightly for him. God help us all to do this! May open eyes, teachable minds, and receptive hearts be ours for that wideness and richness of truth, now discernible, for which prophets, apostles, and Christians from age to age waited, but received it not, "God having provided some better thing for us, that they without us should not be made perfect"!

ITS PASSION FOR MEN.

SYNOPSIS.

The passion for men of Moses and Saint Paul. — This characteristic of fresh thinkers: Throughout the Bible; In Christian ages; In the modern time (examples). — The connection between such thinking and this passion not accidental but necessary. — Consequent war of the newer religious thinking on certain traditional religious ideas inconsistent, as commonly understood, with an adequate view of man, namely: (1) Election and reprobation; the self-sacrifice of the true, Biblical election; (2) Man's sinful state; only most figuratively a "child of wrath;" (3) Worthlessness of works when expressive of character; failure to apprehend the struggle of Christ and the apostles with the Jewish spirit underlies this perversion of Scripture; (4) Man's access to God; this *vital*, rather than analogous to access to the Queen of England; (5) Man's destiny; magnitude of this question; wanted upon it, more light, ampler data, and its re-study. — Consequent war, also, of the newer religious thinking on certain ideas and practices prevalent in society, namely: (1) Merely ease-producing remedies for the evils of society; (2) Superficial remedies; (3) *Laissez faire;* (4) Inordinate wealth and luxury; (5) Asceticism; (6) Unscientific living; (7) The individualistic tendency. — "I will not cease from mental fight."

III.

ITS PASSION FOR MEN.[1]

Yet now, if thou wilt forgive their sin —; and if not, blot me, I pray thee, out of thy book which thou hast written. — EXODUS xxxii. 32.

For I could wish that I myself were anathema from Christ for my brethren's sake, my kinsmen according to the flesh. — ROMANS ix. 3.

IN these words two great typical representatives of newer religious thinking in their time utter the passion of their souls. It is for men.

Moses, stirred by larger religious thought, essays to free his people. "Sirs, ye are brethren," he pleads. Prevented from accomplishing his object, long delayed, but at length entering upon and now amidst his great work, he finds that his people cannot rise to his spiritual ideals, but revert to idol worship and to gross sensuousness. In such

[1] Prospect Street, Sunday night, November 20, 1892.

a case they are repugnant to high moral law, and to God as conceived of under the altogether inadequate category of moral law. In such a plight, when destruction seems awaiting them, and when he himself is tempted to let them perish, and to become in his own person the founder of a truer nation, the God within him offsets the God of his preconception and pleads for his people with this sublime climax, " If [thou forgive them] not, blot me, I pray thee, out of thy book which thou hast written."

Similarly, Saint Paul, the great new religious thinker of early Christianity, would desire to be "accursed," or "separated," or "anathema," for his brethren's sake.

This is one marked characteristic of freshening religious thought. It freed Israel from Egypt. It rescued her anew and anew from her enemies. It led the Hebrew prophets, many of them heretics in their day, to be the most democratic of men, pleading for the poor, the oppressed, the outcast, against wealth, tyranny, and obloquy, — so that they became the forerunners of the liberators of succeeding ages, and by their utterances (together with those of the Hebrew lawgivers, who were actuated by the same spirit) laid as foundations those just principles of human conduct which many centuries later became the basis of the common law, and which have thus come to obtain for the modern world.

Similarly, freshening religious thought broke into the petrified tyranny and cruelty of the Roman Empire, and deferred the overthrow of that empire by Christianizing it; made a way for the tentative rise of free institutions prior to the Reformation; rendered possible, coincidently with the Reformation, far ampler freedom alike for Protestants and Catholics; and is to-day the great humanizing factor in a humanizing tendency which has become so universal that it characterizes many even of those who deny the very grounds for the existence of religion.

In the past century and a half, for example, the fresher religious thinking under Edwards prepared the way for the independence of the American Colonies; and the fresher religious thinking of "Unevangelicals," so-called, like Channing and Parker, and of "Evangelicals," so-called, as seen in a fresher Andover theology, New Haven theology, and New School Presbyterian theology, prepared the way for the overthrow of American slavery, in one of the most gigantic moral struggles of history. So in the mother country, Arnold, Robertson, Maurice, and Kingsley, with many others, some of them passed on, and some of them still living, have been in the forefront of those modifications of the English Commonwealth which have so mightily uplifted and benefited its congested populations.

And to-day the men who are least satisfied with things as they are; who are plunging deepest into social questions; whose life-hold on political economy and on politics is most tenacious, are the men who see a new heavens and a new earth of religious thought and feeling, — some of them within so-called "evangelical" lines; some of them liberals or radicals religiously; and some of them agnostics or unbelievers, but with a freshened and changed religious feeling, whatever their classification. In fact, the men are all about us, who conjoin with fresher and better thoughts of God fresher and better thoughts for men, — Catholic and Protestant, " Evangelical " and " Unevangelical," religious and (as they would call themselves) non-religious, but, in the range that belongs of right to religion, new men, in the new time. "Ring out," they cry, in the lines of Tennyson, —

> "Ring out the feud of rich and poor,
> Ring in redress to all mankind. . . .

> "Ring out false pride in place and blood,
> The civic slander and the spite;
> Ring in the love of truth and right,
> Ring in the common love of good."

The High Church is working for the poor, and so is the Low Church; formal Nonconformist, and informal Salvation Army man. There are the Saint Andrew's Brotherhood man, and the Christian at Work; Toynbee Hall, and Rivington Street College Settlement, and Prospect Union, and the Andover House. Fresher religious thinking, whatever its type, is plunging in, bound to rescue men; while unfreshened religious thought, gathering its skirts about it, too often only offers a prayer, and passes the contribution box. The voice of the latter has too frequently put into polite phrase Cain's question, "Am I my brother's keeper?" The voice of the former, with Moses and Saint Paul, cries to God that it may be blotted out, or accursed, if it cannot do something for its erring, sinning brothers.

I. The first point to which I desire to call attention in this matter is that it is not by accident that a mighty passion for men has attended the newer religious thinking in times past and now, but that there is a necessary connection of cause and effect between them.

Religion is the correlation of man and the Infinite. As, then, men enlarge their thought of the Infinite, the enlargement necessarily goes into the domain of man, as well as of God. God being more freshly, strongly, deeply conceived of, man is by consequence more freshly, strongly, deeply conceived of. The correlation carries them both. If so great, noble, and more and more largely conceived of a being as God is in a relation to men of which religion is the expression, how great, noble, and more and more largely to be conceived of is man also. The one involves the other. Or, to express it more simply: God, we will say, is Father, and men are his children. With the Father goes the child. The child gains in nobility from the Father. New, fresh, strong thoughts of God, then, carry with them new, fresh, strong thoughts of men.

Hence, necessarily, did he who had seen the bush burning but not consumed, and the Sinai glory of God, and he also who had been caught up into the third heaven, yearn alike for the children of so glorious and good a God, and wish to be blotted out, or accursed, if their brethren might not also share the blessing. Or, as Saint John the Revelator put it, reversing the statement, " He that loveth not his brother whom he hath seen, how can he love God whom he hath not seen?" And hence necessarily also did those newer religious thinkers, the Hebrew lawgivers and prophets, become the forerunners of the liberators and of the enlarged laws of mankind.

Hence, too, necessarily did the newer Christianity defer the doom of the Roman Empire, and, yet more and more freshly conceived of, prepare the beginnings of liberty before the Reformation, and give the same in larger degree to Protestants and Catholics after the Reformation, and free our Colonies, and unshackle our slaves, and make the larger liberty of the England of to-day, and spread itself as a reforming and humanizing influence, pervasive as the atmosphere, in this last decade of the nineteenth century. The one involves the other. The enlarging and deepening thought of the correlation embraces the conception of man as well as the conception of God. And so is verified that profound saying of Saint Paul, "Where the Spirit of the Lord is, there is liberty."

II. But, in the second place, the fresher

thought of man, consequent on the fresher thought of God in the newer religious thinking, puts that thinking at war not only with certain current ideas of God, as we saw in the last discourse, but also with certain current ideas of man.

1. The current theology regarding man runs, for example, among men a line of election and reprobation.

True, this is very little spoken of now; but it is unretracted, and lingers as an influencing element in men's thinking. According to this view, the elect are chosen of God for blessing, and the non-elect for cursing. In apparent favor of this view are some Bible expressions, like that about the vessels made by a potter, some to honor and some to dishonor. But from an ampler thought of God it follows that man, his child, is not to be treated in that way. You could not treat your child in that way without running counter to human law, and much more, to the law of God.

That passion for men which characterizes the newer religious thinking presses, therefore, a more adequate study of this doctrine of election and reprobation. From this it appears that the doctrine, as presented in the Bible, occurs there mainly in consolatory passages, as in the eighth of the Romans, where it is urged for comfort and reassurance that God has chosen the reader, and is on his side. From this study it also appears that the chief elect one in the Old Testament is Abraham, chosen that in him all nations might be blessed; and that the chief elect one in the New Testament is the Lord Jesus, who is chosen that men may be saved, and all men drawn to him.

The elect, in short, as another has phrased it, "are elect for the non-elect." Not partialism, but benevolence, self-sacrifice, as in the case of Abraham and the Saviour, and yearning for the good of all, are in this truth.

2. Again, the newer religious thinking cannot regard man so ill as did the older thought.

It thinks as ill of sin as ever. Evil, it is sure, is evil and nothing else. But it conceives of sin more justly. It considers that sin has come from outside influences in part; that blindness is in greater or less degree its cause; and that that part of it — and it is a large part — which is wilful and designing, grows out of a mistaken or insufficient idea of God and of right, even as a wilfully sinning child is such, generally, through not having had its heart touched by love into nobler and better things.

Love, the newer religious thinking knows, can penetrate the hardest heart, afford it vision, stir its aspirations, and mould it, it trusts, into nobler life. Love, in other words, changes the point of view. What law cannot do, a new spirit called into exercise can. Saint Paul has the philosophy of it: "The law of the Spirit of life in Christ Jesus made me free from the law of sin and of death." Accordingly, man being such, and so redeemable, the newer religious thinking realizes, with Scripture, how much that is noble and lovable resides in every human soul. As the Saviour could find it, so this thinking finds it. Fallen indeed is man from the heights he might have attained, of truth, right, and love; but he is still God's child, and only in a most figurative and exceptional sense a "child of wrath."

In brief, the newer religious thinking believes that man, fallen in such a sense, is still nigh to God, dear to him, and in some genuine sense still not fallen, but true, and with something of God in him. This something it sets itself to seek, to love, to develop, and to thank God for.

3. The newer religious thinking deplores also the exaggeration of truth in the old doctrine of the worthlessness of works.

"Not of works, lest any man should boast," says Saint Paul; and his *caveat* ought to explain his meaning. It is a Jewish meaning. The Jew was seeking works as he was seeking gold, to be proud of, and to felicitate himself and indulge himself withal. The more gold, the more pride and ease. The more works, the more pride and ease likewise. Of that kind of goodness, then, the more the worse, since it was assumed for effect, a mere matter of boasting, a thing of the outside and not of the heart. It was upon this false Jewish idea of righteousness that Christ and the apostles flung their lives in protest. The real thing, they contended, was utterly other than this. "Except your righteousness shall exceed the righteousness of the scribes and Pharisees, ye shall in no wise enter into the kingdom of heaven."

What a perversion, now, it is to take this evil, which was peculiar, in great measure local, and the conspicuous trait of a decadent national religion, and formulate from it the doctrine that good conduct counts for nothing! It counts, being real and from the heart, for everything. As clothes put on, as something assumed, it is insincerity, hypocrisy, an object, not for boasting ("lest any man should boast"), but for contempt. But as a real thing, as springing from the heart, as an expression of character, and as in that sense an embodiment of faith, it is precious alike with God and with men. "Thine alms are had in remembrance in the sight of God," exclaims the angel to Cornelius. "I will show thee my faith by my works," writes Saint James.

The newer religious thinking, therefore, while depending in all things on God, and while valuing as beyond price those Christly motives which issue in the noblest living, begs leave at the same time, as it thinks better of God, so also to think better of man, God's child, than longer to undervalue or think lightly of true, heart-inspired good conduct.

4. Nor can the newer religious thinking, though resting alone, in the case of many of its representatives, on Christ as the channel or medium, realized or unrealized, of access to God, any longer believe that access to God is exclusively, as a matter of terms, through Christ.

God is too real, too omnipresent, too immanent in man, for there to be any such literal mediating as the old doctrine assumed. Rather, as many believe, does God in Christ so seek men, whether they realize it or not, that he finds them; and, in their sincere response to his seeking, whatever the form of their response, they have access to God. In some such sense as this, through Christ, whether known by them or not, men find God; but not necessarily through Christ outwardly, in terms, and by way of formality. It might be expressed thus: Christ is the manward side of God. Through him access is thus had. But not formally, diplomatically, forensically, or even, necessarily, as matter of knowledge, but rather *vitally*.

The newer religious thinking ventures, in other words, not to think so ill of man, as God's child, as to suppose that his access to God is analogous to access to the Queen of England. "I was found of them that sought me not," says Scripture.

5. Once more, regarding the destiny of man as God's child, the newer religious thinking begs leave to accept no dictum of mediæval theology, no dictum of a superficial interpretation of Scripture, no dictum not consonant with the whole conception of man derivable from nature, from history, from that charter of religious freedom, if rightly used, the Bible, and from the heart of man under the influence of God's Spirit.

According to the most conservative scientific estimates, man has been on the earth vastly longer than six thousand years, the period set by the old chronology. What was he doing? What was God doing with him? He was unfolding, by slow degrees, on both hemispheres, into being man as we know man. Was God hurling him into hell for that beneficent work, savage though he was? At an analogous stage of unfolding are some peoples now living on this planet. What is God doing with them? Hurling them into hell likewise? Then should good men wish, with Saint Paul, to be accursed with them, to follow them, love them, and, if it might be, to bring them back.

Oh! these questions pressed on us by our enlarging knowledge! What is the destiny of man as a race on this planet? What is the destiny of man, individually considered, after leaving this planet? We can neither, on the one hand, answer these questions with a benevolent optimism, hoping for the best, — because, unfortunately, there is much in the survey which looks by no means toward the best, but toward the worst, — nor, on the other hand, with the theologians of an age which, for frequent offences, burnt people, flayed them alive, and tortured them, can we hasten to remand them to hell torments.

What we want, on this subject, is more light, a re-study of the whole matter, ampler data and more comprehensive generalization. Many are now engaged in this. For myself, while this pursuit is outside the range of my own special studies, I frankly confess that I am unable to resist the hope that God's love will yet find all souls; nor the hope that, here and hereafter, I, in common with all who love him, may be used as a means for his love to find all souls. But neither can I resist the impression that it may be possible for a soul always to withstand God's love. I cannot, consequently, be a Universalist in doctrine. At the same time my hope for the future of every spirit that God ever created is as infinite as God is infinite.

Of the newer religious thinking, then, I may summarily state, that it is devoutly restudying this whole subject, impelled thereto by that larger thought of man which the larger thought of God necessitates; and that, while it is teachable, and feels that it has much to learn, it is at the same time at war with ideas on this subject, long prevalent, indeed, but alike dishonoring to God and man.

Thus in respect to the doctrine of election, of man's sinful state, of conduct when expressive of character, of man's access to God, and of man's destiny, not to mention others, the newer religious thinking is at war with the hard and fast conclusions of an earlier theology; and, while it recognizes much truth in the old positions, and in respect to them, rightly apprehended, is not destructive but constructive, it claims at the same time the right to re-study them, and more justly, reasonably, and honorably alike to God and man, to interpret them afresh.

III. In conclusion I can state hardly more than in propositions some particulars in which the newer religious thinking, because of its passion for men, is at war with society, cries aloud, and spares not.

1. The newer religious thinking does not believe that man lives by bread alone.

Any proposed renovation of society, therefore, by contrivances, like Mr. Bellamy's, to take the hardness out of life, to make everything easy, to have done with the struggle, to have reconstructed society into an organism working with precision like a factory, is, in its judgment, like the holiness scheme in religion, while worthy in more or less respects, substantially a device to construct moral weaklings. Not what we have enjoyed, but what we have suffered, — even as One of old was made " perfect through sufferings," — has probably most benefited you and me.

The remedy must not involve the sacrifice of anything truly educational, tonic, and character-affecting in the present order.

2. Similarly, the newer religious thinking is shy of any proposed remedies for the evils of mankind which ignore the very great complexities of the problem.

The problem is vast. The wisest knows little about it. Man and man's good, which unnumbered ages have only brought to the present stage, are too nearly infinite, having an infinite parentage, and are too little as yet within the range of our comprehension, to be fathomed in a day, a year, a century, or an epoch. That is one of the mighty teachings of the "Idyls of the King": —

> "And slowly answered Arthur from the barge:
>   'The old order changeth, yielding place to new,
>   And God fulfils himself in many ways,
>   Lest one good custom should corrupt the world.'"

The newer religious thinking, therefore, is lowly, cautious, tentative, teachable, receptive in these matters.

3. But, on the other hand, it is not so very meek after all. It has declared war on some things, and will not capitulate. One of them is *laissez faire*.

Every man for himself and the devil take the hindmost is not its doctrine. The older thinking might live along with such a theory, having, under its category of justice, done no wrong; but the newer thinking cannot abide it. Let it, on the contrary, go to the devil with the hindmost, and be blotted out or accursed with the same, rather than encounter the self-condemnation of having had no pity on the hindmost, and of letting him go to the devil with none to help.

It believes that capital has rights; also, that labor has rights. The indifference of capital to labor, in multitudes of cases, it believes to be as wrong in principle as the indifference of labor to capital when it sets costly buildings on fire. When labor destroys capital it does a great wrong, for which it should suffer the severe penalties of the law. But it only does, bluntly and out and out, against capital what capital, by indirect and legal methods and by indifference, frequently does against labor, impoverishing it, crushing it, — yes, and through want and misery often slaying it. The murders wrought, all legally by capital, will, in the eyes of the just Judge, far outnumber the murders by riot and violence which labor has committed; and every one of them will be wicked in the eyes of that Judge.

The destruction of New York Central property at Buffalo last summer by labor, and particularly the interruption of travel over a highway of national importance, are to me simply abominable. But so to me also is that vast railway system simply abominable. Grind the poor, proceed by *laissez faire*, let God's child, your brother, sink whither the miner under the coal combination, and the over-worked railway employee under the railroad monopoly sink, and condemn them for fire and bloodshed? Yes. And if necessary, shoot them or hang them. Before God, they deserve it. But you, ye rich men, ye mighty combinations of moneyed tyranny, proceeding all legally, as our statute books allow, to oppress the poor, — ye, too, are guilty, sinning, moreover, under great light, great opportunity, and great self-aggrandizement. "He that is without sin among you, let him first cast a stone."[1]

---

[1] What is here said regarding capital and labor needs amplification. The spirit of such amplification would be understood by those who heard me. For the reader, I add: —

(1) The corporation referred to is not a sinner above many others. Nor is it, in common with many others, at

4. The newer religious thinking is also at war with the inordinate getting of wealth, and the luxurious enjoyment of it.

Wealth is good, gotten within bounds, rightly acquired, and rightly used ; but to get it beyond bounds, to acquire it by questionable methods, and in any case self-indulgently to roll in its luxury,— this is to sin against what wealth means, namely, untold toil, sweat, and often blood; and it is to sin against the millions who are either starving, or know not whither to look for the next meal.

fault throughout, for it is lacking neither in commendable points of administration, nor in admirable managers.

(2) On the other hand, as regards organized labor, exigencies might arise where violence on its part would be justifiable. The tenet of non-resistance is hardly of universal application.

(3) Having said thus much in qualification of the vigorous language used above, I reaffirm it in the spirit in which I intended it, and as vehemently. For, in this age of the world, and in the light, I will not say of the Gospel, but of those economic principles with which the Gospel is replete, capital has no right, as a matter of economics, other than to work intelligently, obviously, and devotedly for the good of labor ; and a reciprocal obligation, on the same grounds, is laid upon labor. Without their marriage the world cannot go forward. The household which they constitute has no right to be divided against itself. " No man ever yet hated his own flesh."

And that is what this land is doing, — having the most favorable country and government in the world, yet stretching every nerve to outdo the other nations, to see that the products of the skill of the poor laborers of other lands shall not come hither, and to get, get, get, and keep, keep, keep, adding field to field, property to property, trust to trust, monopoly to monopoly, — while the poor man grows poorer, and it is harder and yet harder to get on, and the wretched victims of such a spirit blaspheme the God whom extortioners, in too many instances, profess to worship in gilded temples dedicated to his name. Of this there will be an end and a judgment.

5. It is only just to say that, as the newer religious thinking is at war with luxury, it is also at war with asceticism.

Asceticism is a running away from manful moral conflict. It is bad for the body, which is made for right joys. It is bad for the mind, which needs relaxation. It issues often in calamity to the spiritual nature. Nor is it necessary as a discipline; for this world is hard enough at best, has pain enough, heart-ache enough, trouble enough.

The right and pure use of every good gift of God, and the real self-denial involved in unselfishness, nobility of character, and bravest, truest thought,— these should take the place so long usurped by the artificial self-denial and discipline of asceticism.

6. The newer religious thinking, too, is at war with unscientific living.

In the rich this brings pampering, and too great comfort, and the limiting of families, and presently deterioration. And in the poor this leads to conditions utterly unhealthful, wasteful, and often fatal.

To regard the human body, mind, and spirit, and to regard the environment and conditions of life of these, as a manifestation of a divine wisdom, and discreetly and intelligently, or, in one word, scientifically, to use them,— this is duty; and the contrary, however well-meaning it may be, is sin.

7. To name only one other point, the newer religious thinking is at war with the individualistic tendency.

It was, I think, Maurice, who said, at the time of Wordsworth's death, that he was the last great man of the age that was passing away, — the age of individualizing, introspection, and self-elaborating, however well meant, as in Wordsworth's case, these might be. And he was right, and wrong: right in that with more recent great men the drift is in the other direction, as it is with the time itself; and yet wrong, for the tendency, often indeed beautiful, lives on still.

The newer religious thinking reveres the individual, wishes it all most harmonious development, but knows well that there is only one law of life in this respect; namely, "None of us liveth to himself, and none dieth to himself." Only in realizing and fulfilling this law, in merging one's life into the lives of others, and into, as it were, the corporate life of the community, the State, and the age, can one individually come to the most, or be the most for others. "He that is greatest among you shall be your servant."

Thus in putting little faith either in ease-

ITS THOUGHT OF NATURE, HISTORY, LIFE.

SYNOPSIS.

Threefold category of the world, as Nature, History, and Life. — These a means of perceiving "the invisible things of him." — The newer religious thinking called to confront, not only truth as manifested in the Bible, but truth as manifested in these. — It must listen to the whole oracle, to the whole truth, not to a part of it. — This solemn and momentous, (1) As counter to tradition, and therefore sure to meet with opposition, working various ills, but particularly *within* a man; (2) As tentative, therefore liable to err, and that in matters of the utmost moment; (3) In view of the high qualities of mind and heart which it requires. — But it has received its call and must obey. — Sympathy, love, prayer, fitter to be given it than reviling. — Its reverence for the world under this threefold category. — Bible in hand, it will listen thereto, compare, learn, and derive, no matter by how slow processes, the ampler, better balanced, more rational, more heart-affecting truth. — The Bible enjoins this; its answer to the question, Whither is all this tending? — Attitude, in particular, of the newer religious thinking toward, (1) The widening apprehension of the boundaries of space and time; (2) The widening thought of how life and how man came to be; (3) Other studies, especially those of force and psychic energy; (4) The means, now at hand, for approximating accurate historical knowledge; thus (*a*) What impelled the great migrations? What are the race impulses, Semitic, Latin, Germanic, Celtic, etc.? and (*b*) What testimony for the world has all truly creative literature? (5) Life; this last the ultimate, the test. — "I came that they may have life."

IV.

ITS THOUGHT OF NATURE, HISTORY, LIFE.[1]

The invisible things of him since the creation of the world are clearly seen, being perceived through the things that are made. — ROMANS i. 20.

THERE lies all about us a threefold, wonderful world. In its first aspect, it is the world itself, with its surrounding, shining worlds, with its infinite vast of space, with its cloud-banks of stars, with its awefull distances and silences. These speak to the soul of man with a voice fuller of meaning than any articulate speech. They are the ground facts of our being. They are the background and foreground of existence. In the words of a poet of old : —

> "There is no speech nor language;
> Their voice cannot be heard.
> Their line is gone out through all the earth,
> And their words to the end of the world."

[1] Prospect Street, Sunday night, November 27, 1892.

But this is only the first aspect. The thoughts which you and I have had of the world, others have had before us, and others will have after us. The universe is such that it begets thought, feeling, impulse, action, the ongoing of events, the march of history. The most interesting thing about the sun is not the sun itself, nor its light and warmth, but how it affects the men who behold it. The most interesting thing about the stars is not their distance, their splendor, their value to navigation, their place in the nautical almanac, but how they stir thought. A mountain, a sea view, a winding river, a brook sparkling and laughing through forest and meadow, the glory of a peaceful sunset, all red, and golden, and purple, and amber, the grandeur of dark, frowning clouds, of forked lightning, and of deafening and blinding tempest, — these are not so fine as the emotions which they awaken in the soul, as the impulses which they impart to men, and as their formative influence on individuals and on peoples. What adds an inexpressible tenderness to sea-bordered Ayrshire, to the mountains and tarns of Cumberland and Westmorland, and to the weird Scottish border, is the fact that here were born, and here were developed, men who helped restore thinking peoples, warped off in other directions, to a normal attitude of expectancy and teachableness toward the influences of the world about them. Burns, as another has said, "the greatest lyrist since Pindar," Wordsworth, the high priest of this reverence for nature, and others who moved with them, wrought this for the modern time.

We have, thus, nature itself; and then the thinking and conduct of men, nature-impelled, as they have come down through time, — that is to say, we have history. But there is yet a third aspect of the world; not it itself, nor its unfolding process through men, but present and now, throbbing and responsive, yearning, hungering, aspiring, full of fresh traits, new differentiations, and still awaking powers, — the life of the world. This is the newest thing, newer this year than last year, this Sunday than last Sunday, this moment than the last moment, — life. Life is more than nature; rather, it is nature breathing, feeling, thinking, doing. And life is more than history; rather, it is history brought down to date, and in process of making. And nature, history, life, are the threefold, meaningful substance of the world; so that when the Apostle states for us our principle, saying, " The invisible things of him since the creation of the world are clearly seen, being perceived through the things that are made," he means more than the world itself, or nature; for with nature, and inseparable from it, is what nature comes to, namely, the march of events or history; and with nature and history, and inseparable from them, is what we may call nature alive, or history brought down to date, namely, life.

Thus it comes about that nature, history, and life are the world expressed in adequate terms; and it is these which, as the Apostle declares, manifest forth, as things made since the creation of the world, the invisible things of God, — that is, his thoughts, feelings, purposes, character, " even," as the Apostle adds, " his everlasting power and divinity."

Now the solemn and momentous fact about the newer religious thinking is that it deems itself charged, as the newer religious thinking of no preceding period has deemed itself charged, with the responsibility of confronting not only truth as manifested in the Bible, but truth as manifested in nature, history, and life.

It is sure that truth is truth; that there is no schism in it; that it matches all around; that there can be no authority, even in the Bible, to contravene the authority of God's manifestation of himself in the world. As the prophet who felt himself impelled by a divine command to return at once out of Israel after delivering his prophecy, is represented to have lost his life because he credited a contradiction of the divine command uttered to him by a brother prophet, then lying, and tarried; and as the Saviour rescued from the divine authority of Moses the diviner authority of nature, saying,

"Moses for your hardness of heart suffered you to put away your wives: but from the beginning it hath not been so,"—similarly, in principle, does the newer religious thinking feel called upon to listen to the whole oracle, not to a part of it; to the whole truth, not to a part of it; to the Book of Nature as well as to the Book of Grace; to the whole history of man as well as to the history of Israel; to the present life of the world as well as to that life as it inspired prophets and apostles; and to interpret them respectively in their blended light.

Of the Book of Grace, of the history of Israel, and of the inspired life of prophets and apostles, I shall speak next Sunday night. Of the Book of Nature, of the whole history of man, and of the present life of the world, as they lie before the newer religious thinking, I am to speak this evening.

I. Let me say, in the first place, that this duty of listening to the whole oracle and of hearing the whole truth, which I have characterized as solemn and momentous, is so for several reasons.

1. One of them is that it runs counter to the traditions of many centuries. Galileo suffered for affirming planetary revolutions. Copernicus dared not print his astronomy until about to die. Both were deemed guilty because they would hear the whole truth in their lines of research, not a part of it. One has only to keep his eyes open as he scans the papers, and his ears alert as he walks the earth, to learn that a like guilt is still adjudged the men who will hear the whole truth.

It is solemn and momentous to take such a step. Not only is it not pleasant, but it limits one's usefulness. It keeps a man in America, who ought to be a foreign missionary, — even as I, this week, have received a letter from the mother of such a one, rejected, though from a conservative point of view worthy to go, and though his mother, herself an indefatigable worker for foreign missions for many years, wished to give him, her only son, to the work; the ground of rejection being technically of another sort, but having an inseparable connection with the purpose to hold back men of the newer thinking from the Christly work of bringing the "Good News" to the heathen.

It renders a man working at home the object not only of ill speech, but of vague suspicion and more or less general distrust.

What is far worse, such is psychic action that the person thus limited and hindered, if not well balanced, is apt to be impelled to greater lengths of opinion than would normally be the case, even as persecution begets fanaticism in those capable of it. On the other hand, if the person is well-balanced, so that he keeps a poise and symmetry of opinion, he is apt to be depressed in spirit, and not to develop joyously in his work, as ought to be the case in order to a man's best serviceableness.

In short, not only the guilt judged upon those who dare to hear the whole oracle, and listen to the whole truth, but the unfortunate consequences of it outwardly in limitation of work and restriction of influence, and inwardly in its psychic effect, render this duty of the newer religious thinking solemn and momentous.

2. Another consideration in the same direction is the tentative nature of these new interrogations of truth.

We are only in the beginnings of our ampler knowledge of nature, of history, and of life, and there is large consequent liability to mistake as we study them. So, too, the relative weight, or the correlation, of the two lines of truth is a tentative science, liable to error. Great, moreover, must needs be the ill-consequences of mistakes in matters of so grave a nature. One breaks new ground, sails a sea not yet duly provided with charts, may readily err, and finds himself consequently in tremendously serious business from this point of view.

3. It is tremendously serious business, also, in view of those prodigious studies, of that careful and unbiassed thinking, of that courage and persistence, of that tact and fearlessness, of that thoroughness, and of that combined mental coolness and heart warmth, all of which are required of the newer religious thinking in this aspect of the case.

How little do those who lightly animadvert upon the consecrated Christian scholars engaged in various departments of this one general work realize what qualities must be in these men to start with; what toils, what stresses of mind, and what fortitude amidst evil report, must be constantly exercised by them; and how they are, in this respect, like those who through much pain, loss, and opprobrium have won for the world some of its most precious discoveries, and most gracious emancipations! What an awaking by and by it will be for the maligners of such men to find that, as their fathers slew many a prophet, they have practically been doing the same thing to these! May they be accorded greater mercy then than their eschatology allows!

But there is only one thing for the newer religious thinking to do. It has received its call. It must obey. Counting no cost, shrinking from no peril, dismayed by no arduousness of the task, it must gird up its loins and march out into the untried. To the struggling present, to the unborn future, to the God after whom it hungers, to the men, his children, who are the objects of its holy passion, it must not be found wanting. Think of it, friends, as it prosecutes its task, not with ill will against it as destructive; not with uncharitable thoughts of it, as if it were wilful, wayward, and going forward for the pleasure of it; but rather, with thoughts of sympathy and of love, as for that which is called to solemn, momentous, character-testing responsibility, and is seeking to discharge that responsibility, in the fear of God. Such it is. Let us treat it accordingly. May it be in our prayers. May God bless it!

II. Let me say, in the second place, with regard to the world as comprehended under the categories of nature, history, and life, that the newer religious thinking faces it with reverence and expectation. Here are the facts. Here are the data. It is of God as related to these that the Bible speaks. It is of these as related to God that the world speaks. The two are one book; each is key to the other; each is supplemental to the other; each interprets the other.

What nature is, how it unfolds, what its

types are, what its spirit is, whence it originates, whither it tends, — these are questions best answered by interrogating nature itself. It has a right to testify in its own behalf.

Similarly of the progress of events, or of history. When did man appear on the earth, where, and under what conditions? How did he unfold? Was his original condition that of infantile innocence, followed by a great catastrophe of his moral nature; or is the Genesis account of this matter a spiritualized representation of crises in the individual life? How did institutions originate? Was the order patriarchal, then theocratic, then despotic, then individualizing, or what was the order? Was Israel first under priests and then under prophets, or *vice versa?* In short, of men, of nations, of tendencies, what are the facts? And on the facts what light does the Bible throw? And on the Bible what light do the facts throw? All these are parts of a whole. What is the whole? And what does it testify to us?

Similarly of life now. What is this great load of it which the globe is carrying? —

the blubber-eating, ice-hut-inhabiting Esquimaux, the degraded cannibals, the sombre masses of semicivilized nations, the thronging populations of Christendom, the passions, faults, virtues, hungerings, aspirings of them all? Is our thought large enough, comprehensive enough, teachable enough for all this? Is God manifesting himself in all this, or only in a part of it? And what is life, this flood of energy that emerges into consciousness, that thinks, experiences, feels, loves, hates, and reaches out after some unknown satisfaction, seemingly as various as the individuals are various? Is it an intrinsic thing, individual and immortal, or is it a something that characterizes the mass, and passes away with the mass as that descends to the grave? You and I have each our answer to all this. The Bible affords us strong indications and presumptions regarding all this. But all this, duly studied, answering for itself, and full of meaning and enlightenment for us, is what we want.

Now the newer religious thinking is reverent toward all this, as the work of God; and is full of expectation toward it, as manifesting forth God; and proposes to neglect nothing of it, lest in doing so, it should miss something of God, even as naught was to be omitted from Holy Writ. God, it is sure, cannot disagree with himself. The God in the world and the God in the Bible cannot be two, but must be one. And the newer religious thinking lays its ear close to the heart of nature, close to the phonograph of history, close to the throbbing bosom of life, Bible in hand, to listen, compare, learn, and derive, no matter by how slow processes, the ampler, better balanced, more rational, more heart-affecting truth. And it does so, not only because, like Luther, it "cannot otherwise," but because the Bible bids it to, saying, "The heavens declare the glory of God;" saying, "Consider the lilies of the field, how they grow;" saying, "The invisible things of him since the creation of the world are clearly seen, being perceived through the things that are made."

And if the heart falters; if one asks, "Whither is all this tending?" if it seems as if the old were passing away, and the new were all in uncertainty, then are heard the words, "I have yet many things to say unto you, but ye cannot bear them now;" and the words, "When he, the Spirit of truth, is come, he shall guide you into all the truth." For each age has seen only in a mirror, darkly; the thinking of the past has largely yielded to far better thinking; and as there were ages and orders in geology, each imperfect, each preparative to another, and each passing away, so there are ages and orders of thought, and of religious thought. We apprehend very imperfectly, and the one thing to do is to get all the truth we can, and live it out into golden deeds, and expect ampler truth to break forth, by means of the golden deeds of the present, for the men that shall come after us, and shall be surprised at our limited vision, even as we are surprised at the same limitation in those who have gone before us. "Behold, I make all things new," saith God; and he is ever verifying that word. Let us, then, be well content that this is so, and not borrow trouble, but press fearlessly, truthfully, livingly forward. Not in what is now present, but in that which is to be, shall perfection and finality reside; but it is for us to further that, and to be sharers in its glory by and by.

III. If I have now sufficiently indicated the solemn and momentous nature of the task laid upon the newer religious thinking, namely, to listen to the whole oracle, and hear all the truth; and if I have sufficiently suggested with what reverence and expectation the newer religious thinking is interrogating nature, history, and life, or, in one word, the world, as the work of God, as manifesting forth God, and as able to illuminate the Bible, even as the Bible illuminates it, — permit me to name, in conclusion, certain specific points as characteristic of this newer approach to nature, history, and life.

1. And, first, if we are to admit the objective reality of the universe, — that is to say, if we do not conclude that the universe is only an objectivization of thought or of mind, — space must speak to us in a lan-

guage far more impressive than has been the case in the past; and so must time.

For, on the one hand, the progress in astronomy, the revelations of the great telescopes, the more accurate mapping of the heavens, the better apprehension of the movements of the so-called fixed stars, the story told us by star-dust and nebulæ, and the more adequate apprehension of the origin of such groups of celestial bodies as our solar system, — all these impress the mind with the vastness of space, with the fulness of it, with the seemingly endless cycles of its stellar movements, and with the small part our planet has to play in so great an order, and yet with the mighty persistence of our planet's part in it. And, on the other hand, all this is becoming so much better known, and is so entering into the ordinary comprehension even of children, that its effect on the mind is being greatly extended. The facts, and the apprehension of the facts, in short, cannot but affect our thinking. To the universe, one must believe, there is a unity. One thought is in it; one directing purpose. Of it, as a part, our planet must have been during an unimaginably long past, and, as would seem, must be during an unimaginably long future. The widening boundaries of space thus call for widening boundaries of time, — a thing also suggested by such extremely slow land-making as must have marked the emergence from the ocean of such territory as the peninsula of Florida; a thing suggested by the periods of glaciation on the earth's surface; and a thing suggested, also, by the obviously great antiquity of man.

If, now, space is so great, and time so long, and our earth so little and yet so linked to the greatness and the long continuance of the universe, must it not be evident that the Bible men are speaking to us out of inadequate space and time categories, even as the Saviour warned the Apostles when he said, " But of that day and hour knoweth no one, not even the angels of heaven, neither the Son, but the Father only "? Has not the time been long? And will it not, by all universe and planet indications, be long?

And is not the plan, therefore, by so much the greater? And is it not as extensive as space, and as inclusive? And yet wherein have our systems, shut into the old, imperfect time and space categories, recognized this? These are questions which the newer religious thinking, laying the world Bible and the pen-and-ink Bible side by side, and reverently scrutinizing both, cannot help asking. And with the answer to these questions much else is associated.

2. Then, too, regarding the origin and unfolding of life on this planet, the newer religious thinking "cannot otherwise" than repair to the Museum of Comparative Zoölogy, which its great founder, in his modesty, specified should not be called by his name, but which everybody speaks of as the Agassiz Museum; and "cannot otherwise" than repair to the Peabody Museum of American Archæology and Ethnology, and to like places, to learn how gradually, by what progressive stages, and in what long cycles, animal life led the way to the life of man, and man, in turn, has come to be man as we know him to-day.

Ah! there was an evolution. It is a mere question of detail, relatively, what its stages were. Slowly, gradually, type succeeding type, intelligence more and more predominating, and heart more and more interplaying with intelligence, did life come, and man come, and the man that now is, come to be what he is; and how can we infer, off-hand, that the clock has struck, that we are the culmination of being, that other, larger life is not to succeed? At this great question the newer religious thinking dares to look. It places the two Books, both of God, side by side, — the world Book and the pen-and-ink Book, — and interrogates both and waits for light. And while it lingers thus, awe-struck, amidst its studies, determined to listen to the whole oracle, not to a part of it, it hears again the words, "Of that day and hour knoweth no one, not even the angels of heaven, neither the Son, but the Father only;" and it hears that disciple whom Jesus loved chanting, in old age, as a newer world on this earth was in like manner confronting him, "It doth not yet appear what we shall be."

3. The newer religious thinking confronts in the same spirit other aspects of nature, into which it is impossible now to go, though I cannot but refer to two of them.

One is force, or life, or whatever it is to be called, — the thing alive in nature, the active principle, forceful in gravity, forceful in cohesion, forceful in capillary attraction, forceful in chemical affinity, forceful in electricity, heat, and light, forceful in vegetation, in animal life, in brain life. What is this force? What is this energy? Is it one thing and the same, or is it many things? Has it consciousness in any sense? By what medium is it directed? Is the old category of law enough for it? Has it some sort of volition and power of initiative? Studies in energy, in force, how they stir the soul! How they seem to pierce the veil and show us the invisible!

This is one direction. The other which I will mention is psychic energy. From this platform, not long since, that great psychologist, Professor James, told us some of its wonders. Through what medium does it work? By what processes? What is memory? What are associations of ideas? What part has heredity in it all? The mind, consciousness, processes of thought, powers of inter-mental influence, — toward these, too, as well as toward force or energy, does the newer religious thinking face, Bible in hand, interpreting each book in the light of the other, and bent on hearing the whole oracle, the whole truth.

I have mentioned specifically, thus far, certain aspects of nature only; namely, space and time, the unfolding of life and of the life of man, and, as samples of much more, force or energy, and psychic energy. What is still further to be said relates, first, to history, and, after that, to life.

4. The newer religious thinking hungers, then, for accurate historical knowledge; that it may know how, nature-impelled, life, but particularly human life, has unfolded itself. This, of necessity, must be a mighty commentary on nature as well as on life. And the newer religious thinking is well aware what a shock almost all historical inquiry

must needs be to conventional ideas. For only recently has history been so studied as thoroughly to distinguish between the loose, popular, and often entirely erroneous form which history has taken, and the facts of history itself; so that accurate historical knowledge must often be at variance with popular conceptions. On such studies the newer religious thinking waits for an adequate account of nature brought down to date, and particularly of man. What, it asks, has been the order of events, what the true relations of cause and effect, what the inherent possession of man, and whither his tendency?

(*a*) In this inquiry — strongly suggested to us by the continuous historical impulse of the Old Testament, and by the tendency to historical summary in the speakers and writers of the New Testament — there are two matters of which the newer religious thinking takes special account; namely, the contributions to thought of the different peoples, and of the great spokesmen of the peoples. What, for instance, was it that inspired the great migrations coincident with the migration of Abraham? What impelled the great Indo-European march from the Aryan table-lands of Central Asia, toward the West, until Europe was possessed by it, and it passed on to the New World? What was it, characteristically, that Egypt gave to the world, that Assyria gave, that Palestine and Greece and Rome gave? What is the Teutonic impulse, one side of it forceful through Anglo-Saxons, another through Germans? So of the Celt, the Slav, the Red Indian? All these have a place in that revelation of God which the world is, and, Bible in hand, the newer religious thinking presses these questions.[1]

(*b*) But especially significant in the eyes of the newer religious thinking is all this, as expressing itself in national impulse and in creative literature. The Hebrews came to the front from a national impulse, guided of God. So must all nations have come forward. Therefore, analogously to the

---

[1] For something further on the subject of this paragraph and the next, see Appendix A.

contributions to thought which the Hebrews offered, though of a different importance, one awaits the testimony of all national impulses, —for instance, of that national impulse which found expression in the Arthur legends, and which Tennyson has idealized for all coming time. It is not true alone of men, but also of nations, that there is a spirit in them, "and the inspiration of the Almighty giveth them understanding." In the same spirit the newer religious thinking listens teachably to all truly creative literature. Homer can teach it; the hymn-makers of India; the tablets of Nineveh; the Latin poets; the cycles of the Nibelungen Lied and of King Arthur; Dante and Shakespeare and Milton, and the poets in prose and rhythm of our own age. In a certain quality, none of them touches the high-water mark of the great, constructive Hebrew writers, but all of them have a part to contribute to the expression, emphasis, idealization, and actualization of truth. Therefore, Bible in hand, the newer religious thinking addresses itself to these imperishable aspects of history, bent here, as elsewhere, on hearing the whole oracle and the whole truth.

5. Finally, before life, the newer religious thinking, Bible in hand, sits docilely.

There is nothing like it. One touch of it, as our great dramatist said of nature (using it in the sense of life), " makes the whole world kin." Life, life, life, seen in the smile or the tears of an infant; seen in the laughter and new discoveries of boys and girls; seen in that strange apocalypse, the oncoming of maturity and the dawn of love in young men and women; seen in maturity as it advances through ever fresh stages, new youths, as it were, till the head is white, and the strong limbs totter, and man goeth to his long home; seen in the ever new combinations of the family, of the community, of the State, of the nation; seen in the movements of population; seen in the controversies which agitate society; seen in the mighty enthusiasms which ever and anon seize the world; seen in the march of armies to battle, and in those peaceful triumphs which issue in international arbitrations, in peace congresses, and in the great world's fairs; seen, in short, on every hand, and felt in every heart, and only apprehended by our being ourselves alive, — life, life, life, this is the ultimate, the test, the arbiter, the luminous thing on this globe.

Hence, at its feet, the newer religious thinking sits, Bible in hand still, which tells of One who said, " I came that they may have life, and may have it abundantly." The thoughts which come rolling in upon this thinking it proposes to reduce to life, to test by life, to put to the proof in the conflict of life; and, while it studies the pen-and-ink Bible, also to study the world Bible, in nature, history, life, — sure that he who was "the Life," and is it, wishes the whole of it to be apprehended, appreciated, obeyed, and made alive in Christly living.

"In him was life; and the life was the light of men;" and in like manner all the life which he has touched and inspired — and his touch and inspiration are on and in all life — is also, in larger or smaller degree, the light of men. So believing, the newer thinking presses on in the path, the infinite path, stretching before it forever. Shall not we be of it? Ah! but we cannot help being of it! No man can quite escape from his time. No man can quite shut out the light of God.

ITS IDEA OF THE BIBLE.

SYNOPSIS.

Phenomenal antiquity, survival, and world-affecting influence of the Bible. — Greatly diverse, and yet a unit. — Effectiveness of its form; its *finding* power. — Universality of its hold on men. — It is THE BOOK. — Its influence steadily augmenting. — Anxiety regarding it superfluous and wasted (historical examples). — Reverence of the newer religious thinking for it. — Certain inquiries about it now much at the front: (1) How are the Genesis forewords to be understood? Ecclesiastical ill treatment of them in the past; also in the present ; why the belief is growing that the forewords are a poetic treatment, inspired, and for moral and spiritual ends, of matter derived from a common stock of ancient tradition. (2) Was the order of Israel's life from priests to prophets, or *vice versa* ? Why belief is tending in the latter direction, with the recognition of needful consequent re-arrangement of historical details. (3) The New Testament documents largely original and nearly contemporaneous. But: (*a*) Not enough allowance is ordinarily made for the immediate use for which they were intended; also (*b*) Should they prove less largely original and less nearly contemporaneous, their power for moral and spiritual helpfulness would not be impaired thereby. — The Bible bound hand and foot in the past in certain respects, and needing deliverance. — Its free investigation imperative, and conducive to its highest usefulness. — The book is from God; its light and warmth are eternal.

V.

ITS IDEA OF THE BIBLE.[1]

Every scripture inspired of God is also profitable for teaching, for reproof, for correction, for instruction which is in righteousness: that the man of God may be complete, furnished completely unto every good work. — 2 TIMOTHY iii. 16, 17.

THERE is a book containing fragments of literature probably older than any other literature; a book, in itself and as a whole, among the oldest of books; a book preserved with a care so scrupulous that the variations in its exceedingly ancient manuscripts, though numerous in minor respects, are far fewer than in any other ancient writing of like extent and often transcribed; a book regarded for many ages as sacred; a book the embodiment of that wonderful religious life which marked the Hebrew people, — the embodiment of that thinking

[1] Prospect Street, Sunday night, December 4, 1892.

and history which, in the fulness of time, made a sharp break with the Hebrews, and which retaining what was germinal in the Israelitish religion suddenly emancipated the same from narrowing Hebrew bounds, enriched it marvellously, and gave it, with exulting joy, to become the possession of all mankind.

This book had a most diverse authorship, some twoscore hands at least appearing in it. It sprang likewise out of many ages, and out of vastly different environments and thought-currents. Much of its upspringing, moreover, was out of heated conflicts of opinion, when, from time to time through ages, the old was dying, and the new was struggling to be born. There were great diversities of specific purpose for which its different parts were respectively composed. And yet its many hands, its varied settings and varied age-marks, the successive intellectual and spiritual conflicts out of which it sprang, and the diversities of specific purpose for which its parts were written,—all these have not caused in it confusion, but rather unity, as if still, in different aspects, one and the same thought, purpose, inspiration, was getting for itself expression.

Thus wonderfully a unit, it is nevertheless literature multiform, — history, biography, poetry, parable, philosophy, proverb, law, maxim, and much besides. As regards finish, it is not, in most parts, elaborated to the degree which some literature exhibits; but the plainness, directness, and simplicity gained thereby more than offset any loss in literary form, while it contains many passages as exquisite in this respect as anything even in the Greek tongue. It is strangely able, out of these characteristics, to *find* its reader, to touch his heart, to stir his mind and conscience, to illumine his understanding, and to make him truly wise. Hereby it has entered into the lives of whole peoples, has moulded them, swayed them, and given them laws, liberty, and spiritual momentum.

It has, moreover, been able to affect equally all classes and types of men, — the doubter and the man of intense faith; the man coldly intellectual and the man of great heart fervors; the cultivated and the illiterate; the vile and sinning and the pure and holy; great patriots and great scientists; great statesmen and great inventors and discoverers; women equally with men; the aged equally with little children; those marching into the leaden hail of battle and those studying in the quiet cloisters of universities; those keeping step to marriage music and those bearing the dead to their last home. It has been a comfort alike to sovereigns and to slaves, in palaces and in prisons, to laborers and to the luxurious, to those toiling, sorrowing, despairing, and to those hoping, thriving, successful, — in short, to every human being whom, in whatsoever circumstances, it has reached, and who would let it reach him.

For reasons such as the foregoing, it is THE BOOK, and accordingly it has come about that it bears the name for "book" in the Greek tongue, with the definite article prefixed, and is called, in our dear English speech, with almost the letters corresponding to those in Greek, THE BIBLE.

Nor is the power of this book waning. It is rather steadily augmenting, as it is more and more spread abroad, more and more freed from misconceptions, and better and better understood. Its force is moral, and, as the moral sense is developing, it is more and more *finding* men. It was never read by so many people as are reading it to-day, and never was bearing fruit in so many lives as it is bearing fruit in to-day.

Anxiety is often expressed for its future. Never was anxiety more utterly superfluous and wasted. The Bible has survived crises to which, at present, there is no parallel. It has been almost destroyed from the earth literally, more than once, as, for example, in Josiah's time. It has been buried in inadequate translations, for example, the Latin Vulgate, for centuries. It has repeatedly been hid from the common people, as during the Dark Ages. It has been loaded down with paraphrases and commentaries in past times to an extent which nearly extinguished the book itself. It has been embarrassed by good men's making claims for it which it never makes for itself, and by suffering attacks upon it in consequence, for the making of which there was no just ground. But it lives. Its influence is steadily widening and deepening. It does not need any of our anxiety; it is abundantly able to take care of itself.

The newer religious thinking responds to all this. It reverences the Bible. Those men outside the lines which include you and me, the men who would call themselves of unfaith and of no faith, freely and often express their great regard for it, and, in their way, bear testimony to its benign influence upon them. So of the so-called "Unevangelicals." So of the men outside the boundaries of Protestantism. Men of these different classes, as I pointed out in the first of these discourses, are themselves also in a newer religious thinking ; and their types of such thinking are steadily making, in their respective manners, more, not less, of the Bible. Of the newer religious thinking within so-called "evangelical" lines, in its manner also, the same is true. The Bible was never so much to its men as now. It was never so much to me as now.

From this preliminary statement, I ask you to pass to the consideration of two points: first, certain inquiries about the Bible now much at the front; and, secondly, the sense in which, to the newer religious thinking, the Bible is so much; yes, more even than ever before. And,—

I. Certain inquiries about the Bible now much at the front.

1. The first of these is about the prolegomena, or forewords, of the Bible; those sententious, wonderful passages which brood for us amidst the beginnings of things, and afford us a tender, simple, luminous setting for all that follows after them. How important, for comprehensiveness, background, and symmetry, it is, that the Bible should get some such introduction to its readers, it is easy to see. The question is, How are we to understand these forewords,— Creation, Man and Woman, Eden, The First Sin, The First Murder, The First Civilization, The Flood, The Origin of Diversity in Languages, etc.?

But, first, let it be premised that, among other ill treatments of the Bible, there has been one centring at these very forewords, which the newer religious thinking can never forget. The study of astronomy was long hampered by the old Church interpretation of these passages. This was why Copernicus delayed the publication of his astronomy until he was about to die, and why Galileo was persecuted for affirming planetary revolutions. Similarly, within years more recent, the studies, first of geology, and then of glaciation (so recently as the lifetime of Agassiz), have been hindered by the same understanding of these passages. The earth, it was claimed, could not have been stratified by the causes which geology affirmed, because the six days of creation gave no time therefor; and glacial epochs were alleged to have been superfluous, because the Flood took care of all that. But Copernicus and Galileo, and Kepler and Newton, had their way; and then the great geologists had theirs; and the utterly unwarrantable claims which holy men had put forth for the Bible much to its men as now. It was never so much to me as now.

From this preliminary statement, I ask you to pass to the consideration of two points: first, certain inquiries about the Bible now much at the front; and, secondly, the sense in which, to the newer religious thinking, the Bible is so much; yes, more even than ever before. And,—

I. Certain inquiries about the Bible now much at the front.

1. The first of these is about the prolegomena, or forewords, of the Bible; those sententious, wonderful passages which brood for us amidst the beginnings of things, and afford us a tender, simple, luminous setting for all that follows after them. How important, for comprehensiveness, background, and symmetry, it is, that the Bible should get some such introduction to its readers, it is easy to see. The question is, How are we to understand these forewords,— Creation, Man and Woman, Eden, The First Sin, The First Murder, The First Civilization, The Flood, The Origin of Diversity in Languages, etc.?

But, first, let it be premised that, among other ill treatments of the Bible, there has been one centring at these very forewords, which the newer religious thinking can never forget. The study of astronomy was long hampered by the old Church interpretation of these passages. This was why Copernicus delayed the publication of his astronomy until he was about to die, and why Galileo was persecuted for affirming planetary revolutions. Similarly, within years more recent, the studies, first of geology, and then of glaciation (so recently as the lifetime of Agassiz), have been hindered by the same understanding of these passages. The earth, it was claimed, could not have been stratified by the causes which geology affirmed, because the six days of creation gave no time therefor; and glacial epochs were alleged to have been superfluous, because the Flood took care of all that. But Copernicus and Galileo, and Kepler and Newton, had their way; and then the great geologists had theirs; and the utterly unwarrantable claims which holy men had put forth for the Bible had to be withdrawn, after all the hard words, and the trembling of devout souls, and the humiliating position for a great, comprehensive book like the Bible to be put in, — namely, the position of defence.

And while the newer religious thinking is recalling this, it sees before its eyes the present prodigious studies in zoölogy, in ethnology, and in the gradual unfolding of the race of man on this planet, — studies more recent than those to which I have referred in astronomy, in geology, and in glaciation, which raised such a hue and cry, and against which Scripture texts were hurled; but studies pursuing those same slow, plodding methods of induction by which we came to our present views of astronomy, geology, and glaciation; and as seemingly likely to prove true as they proved true. And here again the newer religious thinking sees the Bible put in the same false and humiliating position, of trying to conquer Darwin by prooftexts, and the godly McCosh by creed-bound professors of Hebrew.

Another fact under the eye of the newer

religious thinking is the Hebrew itself, and its cognate languages; and what the monuments of Egypt and of Assyria, with a great variety of other ancient memorials, have to tell us. From these and other studies it appears that counterparts of these forewords of the Bible were numerous in the early ages, and in a great variety of forms, — Creation, and The Flood, for example. Almost every ancient people had accounts like these, but with diversified details. Which were original? Did the Bible borrow from them? Did they borrow from the Bible? Or did they and the Bible alike draw from a common store of tradition in the possession of antiquity? Of these three suppositions the last — namely, that the Hebrew writers drew, as did the writers of other nations, from a general and common store of tradition — seems to many in the newer religious thinking as the most probable.

Moreover, a comparison of the Hebrew treatment of a particular tradition, and the treatment of the same tradition by the writers of other peoples, reveals the fact that, in each instance, the Hebrew treatment differs from the rest in the accentuation of the moral aspect of the story. For instance, in the very common story of The Fratricide, the other writers make a hero of him, or even a demigod; but the Hebrew account, while indicating his city-building, etc., points out the shame and crime of his bloody deed, — the mark of Cain. These comparisons, together with the seemingly conclusive inference that the Hebrew and the other writers were not drawing, the one from the other, but all from a common store of tradition, lead naturally to the inference that these Bible forewords, instead of being historical and literal accounts of the First Things, were the attempt of holy men of God, "moved by the Holy Ghost," to redeem the common, and often gross and impure, traditions of early antiquity, from such grossness and impurity, and to make them vehicles for conveying moral and spiritual truth.

This inference becomes almost imperative in the attempt of these writers to handle the old traditions about the illicit marriages of demigods to women. This was the common ancient belief. The Hebrew writers on the ancient beliefs could not bring themselves to look at such marriages as anything other than in the highest degree immoral, and yet could not prevent the wide credence of these celestial-earthly unions. What, then, did they? They took, very wisely, the old stories and wrought from them that mysterious narrative in the first eight verses of the sixth of Genesis, where, as they taught, such conduct was so abhorrent to the God of the Hebrews that he repented himself that he had made man upon the earth, and was moved thereby to bring on the Flood. How natural, reasonable, and morally tonic it thus is to see the whole cycle of such tales on the part of the Jupiters of the skies, and the misguided fair ones of earth, dismissed in eight solemn verses, not attempting to controvert the common stories,—an attempt which could not then have been successful,—but branding them as abhorrent to Deity, as causing him to say, "My Spirit shall not always strive with man," as making him repent that

Its Idea of the Bible. 143

he had created man at all, and as issuing in the Flood!

The newer religious thinking, then, while its representatives by no means concur on this subject, and particularly in matters of detail, is greatly inclined, nevertheless, — (1) in view of the great mass of such matter in the early traditions of our race; (2) in view of the improbability, either that the Bible narrative was what the traditions sprang from, or that the Bible narrative sprang from particular versions of the traditions; and (3) in view of the method of treatment in the Bible writers, as for moral and spiritual ends, — is greatly inclined, I say, to believe that these Bible forewords, instead of being historical and literal in the sense of annals, are spiritual and moral, like poems. Similar, though in a far less important connection, is the treatment by which the more or less gross matter in the Arthur legends has been purified, and made didactic of moral and spiritual truth, in Tennyson's " Idyls of the King."

If this supposition is correct, not only

may Copernicus and Galileo, and Lyell and Agassiz, go on with their astronomy, geology, and glaciation, but Darwin and John Fiske may go on with their studies in and philosophizings concerning the origin of man, unmolested. A simple, noble, spiritual account is given, and purpose shown, in these forewords; they make a natural introduction, poem-wise, to the history which succeeds them; and holy men of God are still speaking as they are "moved by the Holy Ghost," "for teaching, for reproof, for correction, for instruction which is in righteousness."

2. There is another question now much at the front. It, and the inquiry about the forewords, are the primary Old Testament questions. It is much the more complicated of the two. But the same simple principle of growing life seems to underlie it. Ah! life is such a touchstone! The question to which I allude is this: Which was prior in the order of time in the life of Israel, the priestly and legal impulse, as has been the traditional view, or the prophetical?

According to almost all historical analogies, the religious life of nations is marked, first, by mighty moral and spiritual impulses, and then by their taking form in law and ritual. But the Old Testament, in the order of its present arrangement, reverses this process. There is, first, very elaborate law and ritual, and then a passing from these to the true inspirers of a people, their prophets and psalmists.

Moreover, enough is now known about the origin of religions; and, in particular, enough is now known about the great Semitic life of which the life of Israel was the most conspicuous part, as well as about the life of Israel itself, — to render it, inductively, highly probable that the order was from spiritual impulse in men like Abraham, Moses, Samuel, and David, to ritual and legal form, from about the general period of Ezra, though having its beginnings much earlier, — a view of the case with which the fearful development of the formal and legal spirit among the Jews in our Saviour's time seems to agree.

This general probability in the case —

namely, that spirit would precede form, and that the mighty spiritual impulse would precede the elaborations of ritual and law, in the shape in which we now have them — is vastly augmented by the relief which such a view at once brings to difficulties that are constantly coming up on the ordinary view. For instance, there had been, we are told, no such Passover as Josiah's since the days of the Judges. But why not, if this was the formal law for all the years intervening? Again, Samuel, not a priest, probably not even a Levite, offered sacrifices. Why did he do that, if the formal law as we have it, which assigned that duty to the priestly class, was then in existence? So, too, numerous reformations in the history of Israel throw up items of detail which are most explicable on the contrary supposition.

I am aware that efforts are made, by one method or another, to explain away all these difficulties, in order to maintain that view which is traditional, and which the surface of the Old Testament seems to justify. But the attempt reminds one of the cycles and epicycles of the Ptolemaic astronomy, by which, on the supposition that the heavenly bodies revolved in a hollow sphere around the earth, it was sought to explain the difficulties in the way of this view occasioned by the seemingly irregular and arbitrary movements of the planets. The moment the Copernican astronomy came in, the cycles and epicycles vanished; the planets were seen to revolve, not in peculiar but in normal orbits; and a whole system of irregularities, until that time ingeniously and variously explained, became no longer irregular, but parts of one vast, simple, and comprehensive working of astronomical principles.

So of the seeming anachronisms and artificialities of the life of Israel. They are capable, indeed, of a great variety of ingenious explanations; but first become entirely thinkable if the writings, as now collected, were, by holy men of God "moved by the Holy Ghost," from time to time rewritten, or re-edited and elaborated, out of a yearning and burning passion to adapt them to the successive needs and exigencies of the moral and spiritual life of Israel.

There would be nothing dishonest, necessarily, in such a course. The people who first heard or read the writings in their newer form would understand it, as we understand a poem or a sermon now, and as a similar treatment of the forewords was probably understood. So far as there were fictions in the process, they would either be legal fictions, like many in constant use to-day, which are neither deceits nor are capable of deceiving anybody; or they would be the analogues of certain writings in the earlier history of Christianity, put forth by men sincerely seeking to serve God, and that, too, not under Old Testament, but under New Testament light.

Such a course would also be true to that law of spiritual life by which knowledge and growth in things spiritual ensue upon effort, and especially effort for others. The disciples who go out to teach in the Saviour's name and to do helpful works, learn and grow as they cannot even by staying with him. He wisely tells them relatively little, and leaves some of the greatest apostolic lessons to be learned in the stress of later work, as Saint Peter's at Joppa, and Saint Paul's in the obscure years in Arabia and Cilicia, and in the failure at Athens which prepared the way for the success at Corinth.

Such a course is called for, as I have intimated, by any quantity of phenomena brought to light in a critical study of the Old Testament. They seem to compel the conclusion that its present state is that into which it was gradually brought through successive attempts of holy and inspired men to adapt its matter to current national needs.

What suffers, if this conclusion stands? Nothing, except our preconceived notion of how the Old Testament came into existence; a notion which the Old Testament nowhere affirms.

What gains ensue, if this conclusion stands? A general induction is confirmed. Difficulties, met as it were by interminable Ptolemaic epicycles, vanish. The growth of the Old Testament becomes reasonable, like apostolic growth. No essential fiction is in the process, but life, warm and unmistakable.

We have first spirit, then form; in short, correspondence to the well-nigh universal law of national and religious unfolding, — this whole vast matter becoming thus amenable to the operations and reign of spiritual law, instead of their inversion.

Here again the representatives of the newer religious thinking are not altogether concurrent, and particularly in matters of detail. They are, however, moving in this direction. They incline to the belief that the life of Israel, as it appears on the surface of the Old Testament, needs re-arranging to agree with facts now ascertained, and in accordance with the laws of spiritual life.[1]

3. Coming to the New Testament, those of you who have perhaps been demurring at what I have said about the Old, will be glad

---

[1] "Needs re-arranging." Not the Old Testament. That is inspired literature, and should remain substantially as it is. Some editions, however, as is beginning to be done, should be so printed as to exhibit the real order of the writings, and, in the case of those books which are composite, the respective elements entering into them, so far as they can be ascertained. "The life of Israel," the rather, "needs re-arranging." That is, it needs to be written, studied, and thought of in its real, rather than in its apparent, order.

to hear me say that prodigious critical studies, relatively new in the Old Testament, have been concentrated on the New for nearly a century, with the result mainly to confirm the historical and detailed accuracy of the New Testament writings. That is to say, these writings are largely original, and nearly contemporaneous. I say, "mainly to confirm;" for there are points on which the highest scholarship still hesitates.

The general result here indicated was to have been expected. For the years covered by the New Testament story were relatively few; the events occurred at the blazing forefront of history; they occurred in what was itself a not altogether uncritical age; and they immediately, as narrated in the New Testament documents, fell into the hands of the great scholars of the second and third Christian centuries, who must have verified them in greater or less degree. On this part of the subject there are only two remarks which I desire to make.

(*a*) The first is, that, while we probably have in the New Testament either documents in substantially their original form, or documents which for substance reproduce original matter, so that, speaking critically, we are treading on somewhat solid ground, we have never enough allowed, on the other hand, for what the Apostle Paul asserts in the text, and implies elsewhere, to have been the purpose of these writings; namely, immediate usefulness.

The Apostle expects the world soon to end. He is writing hurried letters to his convert churches. He so writes as to go back and correct himself without erasure, as in the matter of the persons he baptized at Corinth. He expressly says, in one instance, that he is using his own judgment about a particular case, and thinks he has the mind of Christ.[1] In short, the writing is not for

[1] For a brief, clear, and searching exposition of difficulties attending our traditional approach to the Bible, written by a rare scholar and a rare Christian, see "The Change of Attitude towards the Bible," by Prof. Joseph Henry Thayer, D.D. Houghton, Mifflin, and Company, Boston. 1891.

For an excellent discussion, in some detail, of this whole general subject, see (same publishers and year) Dr. Washington Gladden's "Who Wrote the Bible? A Book for the People."

abstract and scientific purposes, but for immediate and practical use, "that the man of God may be . . . furnished completely unto every good work." He also speaks of his own limitations of knowledge, knowing, as he says, in part, and prophesying in part.

All this suggests to us, what Christ says, that the words he speaks are "spirit and life." Are they not, then, to be taken in their spirit and life, for constructive moral purposes, rather than as arbitrary and hard and fast proof-texts?

(*b*) My second remark is that if the critical studies of nearly a century had turned out the other way, or, by the arrival of fresh historical light, should turn out the other way; that is to say, if it had turned out, or should turn out, that these precious documents belonged to the second century, or the third, rather than the first, the same rewriting and readjustment to the new needs of the Church taking place, as would seem to have taken place in the Old Testament,— if, I say, this had been proved (as has not been the case), or if it should be proved in the larger light of the future (which seems hardly likely), still this discovery would not invalidate the New Testament documents in the matter of their appropriate moral and spiritual teaching, any more than those of the Old Testament on the corresponding supposition.

These writings, in any case, breathe a lofty moral and spiritual life, and that life begets life in men. "The letter killeth, but the spirit giveth life." That spirit, in any event, the New Testament contains to an unequalled degree. And so long as men shall continue to hunger after and be impressible by such a spirit, the New Testament will retain its peerless authority over life. It is not authoritative because certain theological claims can be substantiated for it. As they have all come, so it would matter little if they should all go. It is authoritative, rather, because it has succeeded, as no other literature, in commanding the spirits of men.

II. We now come, in closing, to the second division of the subject, namely: The sense in which, to the newer religious thinking, the Bible is so much; yes, more even than ever before.

The Bible has been bound hand and foot, for several centuries, by what is a comparatively modern doctrine, namely, that of the literal and verbal inspiration of Scripture. I say this is a comparatively modern doctrine, for the apostles quoted the Old Testament loosely, as they could hardly have done, had they regarded its very letters as inspired. They themselves, also, wrote as I have described, which they could hardly have done, had they thought of the letters of the alphabet, and the phraseology which they used, as inspired. Moreover, the writers of the early Church quoted with the same looseness, and, like the apostles, were driving at the point, not the words.

By this doctrine, — comparatively modern, because unknown to the apostles and their immediate successors, — the doctrine, namely, of literal and verbal inspiration, the Bible has long been hampered and mistreated. It was set up to fight Copernicus and Galileo; later, to fight Lyell and Agassiz; at length, to fight Darwin and John Fiske. These positions into which, entirely without warrant, it has thus been forced, have proved, unless we except the last, — and probably the substance of that should be included, — utterly untenable. Similarly, under this same theory of literal and verbal inspiration, it has been set up to fight, with proof-texts, nearly every advance in a profounder, simpler, truer thought of God, which has been suggested since Anselm in the eleventh century, — positions which, in most instances, as in the matter of astronomy, of geology, and of glaciation, have likewise proved untenable.

Now the newer religious thinking does not want the Bible to be subjected any longer to such humiliating work. It is good for something better than the fighting of needless and losing battles. It is inspired, the newer religious thinking believes, in a far nobler way, namely, in spirit rather than in letter. It is inspired for ends spiritual, moral, and practical. Holy men of God, "moved by the Holy Ghost," spake in it "for teaching, for reproof, for correction," and "for instruction which is in righteousness." In the matter of its forewords, of the order of unfolding in the life of Israel, and of the New Testament documents, — in fact, in every respect, — it should be subjected to the same criticism, the same research, and the same interpretation as any literature.

So the newer religious thinking believes, and of this it is not afraid. It welcomes all new light. Just as the new astronomy and the new geology have vastly expanded and illuminated the human mind, so, as these studies advance, it anticipates that the new understanding of history, and the true apprehension of the order and meaning of the Bible documents, will vastly expand and illuminate the human soul. When the Bible is thus freed, when it is stripped of a false mediæval authority and clad in its own pristine authority of spirit and life, it becomes, more even than ever, a new and life-giving book.

And that it is an inspired book, — inspired

by the same Spirit which has inspired all other literature, and has inspired you and me, but inspired in a more conspicuous and life-giving degree than is ordinarily the case with literary or individual inspiration, — the newer religious thinking fully believes. The book is from God. Its light and warmth are eternal. Side by side it stands with that other book, of nature, history, life, of which I spoke last Sunday night. Each throws light on the other. Each supplements the other. Between them, rightly interpreted, there is no schism. Their truth is one. And that truth, it is given you and me reverently to seek after, to receive into our hearts, and to make the lamp of our feet, and the light of our path.

CHRIST ITS CENTRE.

SYNOPSIS.

Importance of indicating the fact of the newer religious thinking. — Obedience unto the heavenly vision its foremost trait. — Its other characteristics have underlying them the principle of a thoroughly enlisted intellect, as well as of a thoroughly stirred heart; the appeal, in short, is to the whole man. — This true even of the practical bent of the newer religious thinking (illustrations). — Hunger after God and passion for men its inspirations; their fine reciprocal relation; their image-breaking but pacific purpose. — The world Book and the pen-and-ink Book its material to work in and grow by; this the highest application of the inductive method; it constitutes an epoch in religion. — Christ its centre: (1) For men outside the faith; in what sense; (2) For "Unevangelicals;" two illustrations; (3) For conservative "Evangelicals" (examples); (4) For liberal "Evangelicals" (examples). — The law of eternal sacrifice. — This the true *In hoc signo vinces*. — This is not getting salvation, but salvation getting us; this is not gaining heaven, but heaven gaining us. — This the divine handwriting on the newer religious thinking. — There is only one thing for you and me to do, namely, to throw ourselves into this infinite Christ principle.

VI.

CHRIST ITS CENTRE.[1]

Who, being in the form of God, counted it not a prize to be on an equality with God, but emptied himself, taking the form of a servant, being made in the likeness of men; and being found in fashion as a man, he humbled himself, becoming obedient even unto death, yea, the death of the cross. Wherefore also God highly exalted him, and gave unto him the name which is above every name; that in the name of Jesus every knee should bow, of things in heaven and things on earth and things under the earth, and that every tongue should confess that Jesus Christ is Lord, to the glory of God the Father. — PHILIPPIANS ii. 6-11.

I UNDERTOOK, in the first of these discourses, to indicate the fact of a newer religious thinking, and to characterize that thinking.

It is important to indicate the fact, — not unduly, not out of proportion, especially not

[1] Prospect Street, Sunday night, December 18, 1892. Down to the paragraph beginning, "It is to this point, then, that we now come," on page 171, I have substituted a differ-

in neglect of much else of large importance, and, particularly, not in neglect of simple, every-day duty, thought, and devotion. But, assuming that due proportion is maintained, this great, present-day fact needs making known. The ostrich, hiding her head in the sand upon the approach of peril, is not a wise bird. Neither, unless in appearance, is that bird wise which, when all the woodland is carolling the glory and joy of the dawn, hides from it in some cleft of tree or of rock. To know one's time, to apprehend its perils and possibilities, to feel with quick and tender sympathy the heart-throb of its great aspirations and inspirations,—this is to live. Its contrary is to fall under our Saviour's surprised and pained rebuke, "Ye cannot discern the signs of the times."

In characterizing the newer religious thinking I spoke of its spring in "heavenly vision," and its obedience thereto. That is

ent opening of the discourse from that used in preaching it. I have also permitted myself an anachronism of two days in the illustration taken from my own parish on pages 165 and 166. For the original opening, with the reasons for the transposition, see Appendix B.

its most important trait. No prophet of old was ever more truly moved of God than the best spirit in this thinking. And the very obloquy which it is sure to encounter, chastens and makes higher than of this earth the holy resolution with which it presses forward. I can only repeat what I stated as I drew attention to the point: " Let no man say, or even imagine, that this thinking is other than inspired by, and obedient unto, a 'heavenly vision,' which ever hovers in its foreground, and beckons it on."

The other characteristics which I named were: "its scientific temper;" "its practical bent;" and "its purpose to include in its concept the entire religious impulse of the world."

One principle underlies all these. It is the principle of a thoroughly enlisted intellect, as well as of a thoroughly stirred heart. This is the glory of the religion of the new time. It appeals to the whole man. There is no servility of a half or two thirds of the man to the other half or third.

Take, for example, what might seem an

exception to this, namely, the "practical bent" of the newer thinking. One might point, with this in mind, sneeringly at the thinking, and say, " It may do for professors and essay-preachers, but practical men don't care for it." But he would have reflected little who should so employ this trait. The fact is that many of the most practical Christians, to-day, are practical, as a sheer intellectual necessity. They cannot abide the idols still standing upright in the imagery chambers of traditional theology. Neither, on the other hand, can they give up their hold on God. Therefore they turn, almost desperately, to work. Here they will find, they are sure, light. "If any man willeth to do his will," they console themselves, "he shall know of the teaching." I adduce two illustrations of this.

When the profoundest theologian of our century, Maurice, was spending his days and nights for the London workingmen, and in that work *discovered* Charles Kingsley, Thomas Hughes, and many another, it was the intellectual necessity of something practical, not less than sympathy for the men needing help, which became the key to that remarkable chapter in our century's history. This, and, so far as we can see, this alone, gave Charles Kingsley and Thomas Hughes not only to literature, but also to the intellectual enrichment of our century's religious life.

But to come nearer home. There listened eagerly to the earlier of these discourses a physician, second to few in this Commonwealth as a general practitioner, who, the last two nights he was out, spent them devising ways for increasing the practical efficiency of this church; who, with pneumonia upon him, answered, nevertheless, a night call the second of those nights, and desired to start out in the morning; and who, ten days thereafter, was with the great Physician. His hands and his heart were ever full of all sorts of practical helpfulness to men. And his last testimony in our meetings was in a vein of rejoicing that creed-wars were waning, and that the Christian Church was getting to work. And what was he? A man of deepest, tenderest sympathies? Yes; but also a man of doubts, questionings, perplexities, who at once conquered them, used them, and became a humble servant of the Lord Jesus through practical work.[1]

The practical bent, then, as well as the scientific temper, and the purpose to comprehend and utilize the truer impulses of all religions, noticeable as traits of the newer religious thinking, indicate, all of them, as I said, the thoroughly enlisted intellect, as well as the thoroughly stirred heart. The whole man, in short, is coming to the front in religion. Is not this significant? Does it not betoken a new time? Ought it not to make our hearts sing?

But the measure of a movement is in its inspirations. We saw the fact and some traits of the newer religious thinking in the first discourse. It was in the second and third that we saw what its inspirations are. They are the highest, the noblest, — hunger after God, and passion for men. Not since

---

[1] Dea. David Marks Edgerly, M. D., truly a "beloved physician." Born, August 11, 1839; died, December 20, 1892.

Christ was in the flesh has a movement in religious thought been more thoroughly imbued with either of these impulses; and the most blessed aspect of the present movement is that they are in such fine balance, each equally present, and each giving symmetry and glory to the other.

We saw, also, how these impulses lead inevitably to a certain image-breaking, in Godward and manward theology not only, but also in the life of society. For the "stone cut out of the mountain without hands" is to "break in pieces and consume" not only the image of Nebuchadnezzar's dream, but all images. It has not come "to send peace, but a sword." It ought not, however, to be thought of as a conquest, but as, the rather, a measureless love, with its end peace. Happy will it be for us if we shall capitulate with it early.

Having these noble and so reciprocal inspirations, and this at once destructive and constructive work in hand, has the newer religious thinking adequate material to work in and grow by, or is it a kind of wild passion of the age, like the crusades, which were utterly barren, except in their indirect results? You remember how the wise Arthur deprecated for most of his knights the quest of the Holy Grail:—

> "Go, since your vows are sacred, being made:
> Yet — for ye know the cries of all my realm
> Pass through this hall — how often, O my knights,
> Your places being vacant at my side,
> This chance of noble deeds will come and go
> Unchallenged, while ye follow wandering fires
> Lost in the quagmire! Many of you, yea most,
> Return no more."

Is the newer religious thinking such a quest, or has it adequate material to work in and grow by?

The fourth and fifth discourses afforded us the answer to this most serious question. We saw that the unique distinction of the newer religious thinking of the present is its being set to read two books, not one; to listen to the whole oracle, not to a part of it. Whereas, before, mainly only one book has been read, and only one philosophical method followed, namely, deduction, we saw that induction is now to take its appropriate place along with deduction in the work of this thinking, and that that other God's Book, nature, history, life, or, in one word, the world, is now to be laid side by side with the pen-and-ink Book, the Bible, and each made to interpret the other.

This change in philosophical method; this recognition of the larger handwriting of God, —

> "And Nature, the old nurse, took
> The child upon her knee,
> Saying: 'Here is a story-book
> Thy Father has written for thee.'
>
> "'Come, wander with me,' she said,
> 'Into regions yet untrod;
> And read what is still unread
> In the manuscripts of God;'" [1]

this sublime purpose to find God in his whole universe, and to let him speak to men out of his whole universe; and this arduous task of rethinking everything into the larger terms of God as so manifested, — constitute an epoch in religion not less momentous

[1] Longfellow, "The Fiftieth Birthday of Agassiz."

than was constituted for science when it gave itself to the Baconian method. In fact it is that method, given its highest application. The other method in religion, in point of fact, was too often only a kind of quest of the Holy Grail, following "wandering fires lost in the quagmire." Employing this better method the quest is becoming substantial and real, with promise of results more reasonable and permanent.

Thus, from the indicating and characterizing, through the splendid inspirations and tasks, and then through the new and magnificent material and method, we are come, for the newer religious thinking, to this crucial inquiry: What is its centre? Indeed, has it a centre? Is there any Arthur, in his Hall of Camelot[1] (for this seems the mean-

[1] This was how Camelot looked as men approached it, eluding and yet winning them, and drawing them within itself: —

> "Far off they saw the silver-misty morn
> Rolling her smoke about the Royal mount,
> That rose between the forest and the field.
> At times the summit of the high city flashed;
> At times the spires and turrets half-way down
> Pricked through the mist; at times the great gate shone
> Only, that opened on the field below: . . .
> And there was no gate like it under heaven."

Christ its Centre.

ing of the "Idyls"), for it ever to come back to, and ever to start out afresh from, and ever to live under the vow of?

Blessed be God, there is! It is that mysterious Person, of whom the mystery of Arthur's "Coming," and "Passing," and wondrous defeated and yet triumphing life, seems to be speaking to us. And we grossly wrong the mystery, — mysterious from any point of view, — if we seek too deeply to penetrate, or too precisely to define that Person. That was how they treated Arthur, — some denying that he was what he claimed to be; others maintaining that he was more than he claimed to be; none compassing his practical meaning for life; and even his last knight fain to deceive him in the matter of his dying request. Ah! what an epic is that of Tennyson's! Would it might teach us!

It is to this point, then, that we now come in closing; namely, to note that Christ is the centre of this movement.

1. I wish to indicate this, first, in regard to many men outside the Church altogether,

the earnest doubters and unbelievers, who, as we saw in the first discourse, are also in a movement, an advance, which differentiates them from the like type in earlier periods, so that the true men among them are more earnest and reverent, and are pained not to believe.

We are told that, as Jesus hung upon the cross, it was where many passed, and that they looked on him, and that some, even among those farthest from the faith, were touched; for example, the Centurion. I should like to follow the lives of those who saw him, and observe if they were not permanently affected by the sight. Christ said he would, if lifted up, draw all men unto him. I wonder if this saying of his did not begin to be fulfilled while he hung there on the cross. It is so, at any rate, with the men of whom we are now thinking. Jesus of Nazareth, whom they do not confess to be Jesus also of the skies, has his hold on them. Of course it is not just the hold he has, I hope, on you and me. Would God it were an ampler hold on them; yes, and on us, likewise! But, of its kind, it is as real as on you and me,— if not as adequate, at any rate as real. Let us see how this is.

There have been certain figures in history from which the world never has been able to get away. One of them is composite, the figure of the old Greek life, shown us by wonderful Homer. Whatever person, and whatever civilization, has beheld this composite portrayal of antique life, will never be the same, after the sight, as before. So, too, specifically, of the figure of Socrates, or the figure of Dante, or the figure of Martin Luther, or the figure of William the Silent, or the figure of Shakespeare.

Now like these, only vastly deeper, more acute, more potent in influence, more constructive of life, is the figure of Jesus, with these men. Homer gives a composite, universal expression of the antique; Socrates, of the moral,— of truth-seeking, inward-voice-obeying, spiritual intelligence; Dante, of lofty spirit, betwixt the old world and the new; Luther, of the Germanic impulse, and of its emancipation into spiritual liberty;

William the Silent, of the spirit of tolerance and freedom and comprehension; Shakespeare, of the heart of man in all time.

But not one of these approaches the significance of the figure of the Lord Jesus, nor do all of them. There he is. There he depends from the cross. One cannot say ancient or modern of him, for he is of all time, as appropriate to Homer's age as to the age of Augustus, as appropriate to the age of Victoria as to the age of Dante; in fact, dateless, timeless, a being belonging to the forever. One cannot associate him with Socrates, for he is morally much vaster than Socrates; nor with Luther or William, for they are only tapers from him; nor with Shakespeare, for he knows all that Shakespeare knows, is vastly more universal, being Semitic as well as Indo-European, and, where Shakespeare gropes in the dark, as in the Sonnets, he is all light, as in the fourteenth to the seventeenth of Saint John.

Now this universal figure, this Man of sorrows depending from the cross, is there, — there and unremovable; and, being now universally diffused abroad, through the lives of him, the comments on him, the universal impression of him, he is swaying these men, — swaying them by the power of his transcendent character, his unequalled sayings, and the *tout-ensemble* of his personality. To his thoughts these men bow. To his conceptions they more and more adapt their lives. He has softened their scoffing. He has made them tender and earnest. They do not acknowledge, as we do, his Deity, but they bend to his character.

And thus it comes about, in peoples that know Christ, even though many among them are ungodly, that the Christ-thought gets the upper hand; that complicated elections simplify themselves; that an aroused public conscience registers the verdict of the Lord Jesus; that great tyrannies fall down; that great wars come to the right end; and that the King of kings, in the person of our Lord, goes forth to every conflict with no uncertainty what the ultimate outcome will be.

It would be easy to establish what I have

affirmed from the sayings of men of this type, but I have enough suggested the proof. Of the truer spirit outside the faith, Christ is the centre. Already it is under his resistless eye. Already it swings, however unwittingly, to his bidding.

2. The same is true, with augmented force, of those in the Church, but outside so-called "evangelical" lines. And the augmented force lies in this, that, while, in distinction from you and me, they deny the true Deity of the Lord Jesus, they regard him as very specially related to God.

In him, they say, God has most perfectly manifested himself. There is a divine mystery, they affirm, about this wonderful being. Him they count their Saviour, their leader, their glorious exemplar. They do not go as far as we. We are sorry they do not. But they go a good distance. They accept him as Master. He marshals them. He directs them. Now these men, as I have earlier pointed out, are in one section of the newer religious thinking; and, in their newer thought, Christ is central, — his character,

Christ its Centre.

his way of helping men, his simplicity, his incisiveness, his lofty and tender spirit. If afar off, as some of us would say, they nevertheless follow Jesus. Yes, and perchance, many a time, nearer than we.

I have met personally with two affecting illustrations of this within a few days. A young minister of a " non-evangelical " body, consuming with zeal, love, service, introduced me to an aged parishioner of his, and left us together. Then began this old man to testify, almost with tears, to what this young man was doing for him and for his church. " We never had," he said, " such a minister. There was never a minister that did so much for me." Why? I knew why. He never had had a minister who so completely, however defective his doctrine, lived as in the presence and power of the Lord Jesus.

The other illustration was in a well-stocked private library. I took down a book bearing on the life of the Lord Jesus. Struck by it, I asked my host what he knew of its author. " He is an Englishman," replied my friend, " ' non-evangelical,' an advanced man. I visited him when I was abroad. He is a great scholar, a great thinker, but, like Martineau, most devout. His home suggests an oratory, redolent of sanctity and prayer."

Here, then, were a young New England pastor, of one "non-evangelical" denomination, and a great English scholar of another, the doctrinal deficiencies of both of whom you and I would regret; but both of whom were not only under the general moral influence, as in the case of men outside the faith, but also under the personal and spiritual power of the Lord Jesus Christ. The examples are typical. They suggest, out of life, my point.[1]

3. Without going into other divisions of the Church, I come now to "Evangelicals," such as we. And, first, those of them who

---

[1] One has only to think of Dr. Edward Everett Hale, the author of "In His Name," and of Dr. Andrew P. Peabody (passed on March 10, 1893), who was as devout and tender a disciple as the Saint John he loved so well, to understand how truly Christian, in the New Testament sense of that word, are multitudes whom those who claim to be more acceptable Christians than they, have so far forgotten the spirit of Christ as to pronounce "unevangelical." (See pp. 208, 209.)

have little responsiveness to the freshened religious thinking of our time.

Conservatives, we should call them. But some of them are, along practical lines, mightily parts of a progressive movement. The dead Spurgeon is an example. Very conservative in theory, in practical directions he was radical, — pushing for new methods, new appliances, new instrumentalities, building up his great Metropolitan Temple work, his Lay College, his Orphanage, etc. The living General Booth, of the Salvation Army, is another example. Book after book falls from his pen. The drum-beat of the army associated with his name, like the drum-beat of the army of England, follows the rising sun around the world. Dwight L. Moody is another example, — fearless, hospitable, asking Professor (now President) Harper, who so much disturbs some people about the Old Testament, to speak at his Summer School.

Conservative men are all these, and many another, yet advancing men; mainly advancing in practical directions, it is true, but parts of the great world movement. Need I ask who inspires them; who is central to their progress; who is the Leader, Captain, All-in-All of the Spurgeons, Booths, Moodys, and those of like temper, in the great marching army of Christian workers of this type? It is he with the thorn-marks in his brow, the nail-prints in his hands, the spear-thrust in his side.

4. And next, and finally, we come to those members of "evangelical" bodies, to whom I have made repeated reference, who, in intellectual as well as practical lines, are parts of the newer religious thinking.

They are the Coleridges, the Arnolds, the Robertsons, the Maurices, the Kingsleys, the Bushnells, among the dead. They are the Farrars, the Phillips Brookses,[1] the Heber Newtons, the T. T. Mungers, the Washington Gladdens, the Lyman Abbotts, the Egbert C. Smyths, among the living. They

---

[1] Dead, alas! January 23, 1893. But never so alive as now, on the earth as well as in heaven. "It is expedient for you that I go away."

have little responsiveness to the freshened religious-thinking of our time.

Conservatives, we should call them. But some of them are, along practical lines, mightily parts of a progressive movement. The dead Spurgeon is an example. Very conservative in theory, in practical directions he was radical, — pushing for new methods, new appliances, new instrumentalities, building up his great Metropolitan Temple work, his Lay College, his Orphanage, etc. The living General Booth, of the Salvation Army, is another example. Book after book falls from his pen. The drum-beat of the army associated with his name, like the drum-beat of the army of England, follows the rising sun around the world. Dwight L. Moody is another example, — fearless, hospitable, asking Professor (now President) Harper, who so much disturbs some people about the Old Testament, to speak at his Summer School.

Conservative men are all these, and many another, yet advancing men; mainly advancing in practical directions, it is true, but parts of the great world movement. Need I ask who inspires them; who is central to their progress; who is the Leader, Captain, All-in-All of the Spurgeons, Booths, Moodys, and those of like temper, in the great marching army of Christian workers of this type? It is he with the thorn-marks in his brow, the nail-prints in his hands, the spear-thrust in his side.

4. And next, and finally, we come to those members of "evangelical" bodies, to whom I have made repeated reference, who, in intellectual as well as practical lines, are parts of the newer religious thinking.

They are the Coleridges, the Arnolds, the Robertsons, the Maurices, the Kingsleys, the Bushnells, among the dead. They are the Farrars, the Phillips Brookses,[1] the Heber Newtons, the T. T. Mungers, the Washington Gladdens, the Lyman Abbotts, the Egbert C. Smyths, among the living. They

---

[1] Dead, alas! January 23, 1893. But never so alive as now, on the earth as well as in heaven. "It is expedient for you that I go away."

are, at once as practical men and as intellectual men, in the newer religious thinking. They have their faults, perchance their errors. But to their voices the voice of the souls of sinning, fallen, needy humanity responds.

And there is but one centre to their thinking and their work, — namely, the Crucified One. Believing that he was in the form of God, but counted it not a thing to grasp after to hold equality with God, but, the rather, emptied himself, took the form of a servant, was made in the likeness of men, humbled himself, and became obedient to death, even the death of the cross, — they hold him therein to have impersonated, as in no other way it could be done, the great heart of God; and that therefore, not so much because he was God, though he was God, but because in flesh and blood he embodied the infinitely sacrificial heart of God, "God highly exalted him, and gave unto him the name which is above every name;" and "that in the name of Jesus every knee" shall "bow, of things in heaven and things on earth and things under the earth, and that every tongue" shall "confess that Jesus Christ is Lord, to the glory of God the Father."

This is their conviction, this their faith, this their inspiration. Along this line they are moving. God is God, they believe, and Christ is God, not so much because they are God, though they are that, but because they are God-like,— self-emptying, sacrificial, spending and being spent for others, for men, and for the spirits above and beyond men. Here they see God resting his highest claim, and Christ his highest, not in Deity *per se*, though they are that, but in God-like love, sacrifice, self-emptying.

A universe could not be called into being, these men remember, without infinite suffering. This infinite suffering, God,— this infinite suffering, Christ,— these men remember, was ready to undergo, and thus to be, as it were, " slain from the foundation of the world." Human beings, and other spiritual existences, could not be called into being — any more than the coming into being of a family of children is possible —

without immense suffering, and immense sin as the sequel. These, too, God,—these, too, Christ,—was willing to undergo and endure. This self-emptying and self-forgetting — as is slightly suggested by the self-emptying and self-forgetting of a parent — did God, and especially God in Christ, make the law of the Divine Being. Therefore, by highest right, God is God; therefore Christ is highly exalted, and given "the name which is above every name."

Do you catch the thought? Do you see how far-reaching it is? "God is love." "God so loved the world." God's claim is based there. God's command of us is fulcrumed there. Not on sovereignty, though there is sovereignty enough; not on law, though there is law enough; not on right, though there is right enough; not on justice, though God is just; but on love,—the love of an infinite and eternal sacrifice, penetrating the world, pervading it, conquering it, lowering its proud look, bringing down its lofty head, turning it as the rivers of water are turned. Love is the clew; love is the key,— and love running through everything: through nature, making it sacred; through history, hallowing it; through life, imparting to it a new meaning, so that light comes, freedom comes, growth comes, yea, the new heavens and new earth, wherein dwelleth righteousness.

Constantine, on the eve of battle, seemed, as everybody knows, to see in the sky a cross, and the legend, "In this symbol conquer."[1] In it he did conquer. But little did he guess, or did the Church of his age, or of the succeeding ages, guess the full import of the symbol. The full import is the eternal sacrifice in the heart of God. Of this import our age, enabled thereto by its mighty enlargings on every side, is, for the first time, getting some adequate glimpses. To its power this age is bending,— love, the cross, the infinite sacrifice in the heart of God, emulated in the hearts, the thoughts, the lives of men. And, as if it blazed before the sight of men in every sky, it is saying, "In this symbol conquer,"— breaking down all oppressions, righting all wrongs,

---

[1] Strictly, "thou shalt conquer."

bettering steadily a world so in need of betterment, lifting life into higher thoughts, nobler ideals, loftier conceptions, more adequate realizations and completions, under the lead of the Crucified, — he the centre, he highly exalted, and, in some sense, all knees bent to him, and all tongues confessing him.

This is more than getting salvation, though it is salvation. It is salvation getting us. This is more than gaining heaven, though it gains heaven. It is heaven gaining us, — gaining us over to its ruling idea, filling us with it, transfiguring us by it, and making it to be true that we, his servants, both here and there, serve him, and have his name in our foreheads.

Here it is that the newer religious thinking, — not mine, not yours, not any man's, not perfect either, but still faulty and inadequate enough, — along the pathway of which God is leading the world, and of which I have sought to say something to you these closing Sunday nights of the year, shows upon it the divine handwriting, being from

Christ, and centred in him, and moving toward him.

And there is only one thing for you and me to do,—a thing which, at the best, we never have enough done yet,— namely, to throw ourselves into this infinite Christ principle, into this infinite law of the spiritual kingdom, into this divine imperative of the universe, and to become the very children and personal presentments of the cross. He who therefrom depends, leads, and ever will lead, turning and overturning, conquering and to conquer, and renewing evermore — even as it is written, " Behold, I make all things new " — thought, feeling, life, yea, even you and me. To him be the glory, both now and forever. AMEN.

APPENDIX A.

ONE TYPE OF NATURE TEACHING.

NOTE.

At the point in Discourse IV. (page 124) whence reference is made to Appendix A, I have spoken not only of the testifying power of nature indirectly and in general ways, but of its more direct voice. What, it was asked, are those impulses of peoples, those movements of them, those peculiarities which give them each, as it were, a vocation and a distinctive message for the world? "All these," as was there said, "have a place in that revelation of God which the world is."

To illustrate this subject in a single direction, I append the closing observations in an address of mine before the New England Water Works Association, given in Boston, December 12, 1888, entitled "Water in Some of its Higher Relations," and printed in the Association's "Journal" for March, 1889. The last paragraph, not in the address, but added as a note when it was printed, is here brought into the text.

Nature being of God not only, but God being in nature, and speaking through it, when shall that great heresy be arrested by which the two are put in antithesis, and by which nature is so demeaned as at best only now and then to be summoned into court "evidentially"? When shall its holy voice on all sides of us be simply and livingly heard? Children so hear it, — "the greatest in the Kingdom of heaven." So do the poets, — succeeding, as they know how to, in remaining children always. We must come to their place, or miss much of the sweetness, depth, and glory of God.

ONE TYPE OF NATURE TEACHING.

IF this seems fanciful to you, this mighty impulse of descending streams, of great rivers, of sparkling archipelagoes, and of bordering seas, in giving a type to national life, and in helping set forward world-historical movements, I ask you to think of two or three more modern instances.

What, then, let me ask, was the Anglo-Saxon fatherland? It was Teutonic. Why, then, do our brothers of Germany, and of the Low Countries, stay mainly on their own soil, or colonize only feebly, while we ourselves, having been first transferred to the mother Islands, have colonized the world, are erecting mighty nationalities on three continents, and are giving to the whole world our institutions and our speech? Before you answer this question I ask you to sail along the shores of the Continent, opposite Great Britain; to note that there is hardly a respectable natural harbor on the French coast; to note how remote and difficult of access are the better harbors of the North Sea and of the Baltic; and then, crossing the Channel, to observe that our mother Islands are fairly fringed with bays, inlets, safe harbors, and inviting river mouths. Sail up the Irish coast, for example, with this distinction in mind. The whole coast configuration, the whole maritime quality of these islands, were a perpetual predisposition to the sea, to its hardy employments, to its openness of mind, to its far-reaching adventure. Water, and the water impulse and opportunity, are the answer, physically, to the question why the Anglo-Saxon civilization, which, indeed, had within itself elements mightily adapted to the same end, is erecting great nationalities on three continents, and is imparting its spirit to the world.

But let us keep within the lifetime of our own generation. Go back, in our own country, to 1860. Why was it, in all the stress and conflicting sentiment of that stormy period, that North and South did not separate, like Abram and Lot dividing the land? One great reason, one conclusive practical reason, one unanswerable argument to multitudes who would not have stood upon theory, was the simple natural fact that a mighty river coursed from north to south through the alienated sections; that the natural flow of waters, and the natural dip of water-sheds, pointed out that this ought to be one land, not two; and that it was impracticable for it to maintain itself as two.

Or go back to 1870. There is a magnificent river, almost a second Rhine, descending from the southwest by a northeasterly course to the Rhine, and joining it at Coblenz, namely, the Moselle. The two streams are, for all practical purposes, one. The country drained by them is the same in character. The Moselle belonged within the old German frontier. All the Rhine love was shared by it. But France had claimed and held the Moselle. The struggle of 1870 came. Then the old river passion awoke. That fair valley was wrested back. In the great German national monument, far up on the heights overlooking the Rhine at Bingen, where colossal bronzes have been erected as a memorial of the uprising and unification of the German peoples in that war, one member of the group is a figure representing the Moselle, won back to its sisterhood with the Rhine. But the river love and the river spirit, expressed thus in bronze, were even realer and more constructive than the statue indicates in that fierce national struggle.

The final higher relation of water which I mention is one difficult to be defined, and of which I can take time to give only two illustrations; but it is as real and mighty as any of the others. I refer to *the power of water on the human imagination*. And I think I need hardly contend, before a company as intelligent as this, that genuine and profound influences on the imagination are among the most powerful springs of human conduct.

I ask you, then, first, to think of the Arthurian legends. There is a great mass of them. Their principal home is the British Isles. Their constructive thought is, the reappearance of Arthur, in the ages to come, to bring in days better even than the old days of that king and of his Table Round. They have been cast into perhaps their best practical, as certainly into their most poetic, form in Tennyson's "Idyls of the King." Any one who has studied them, and who is at all familiar with the spirit of Anglo-Saxon history, will, I think, admit, that they well typify the best movements of that history; that they are true race legends; and that much of their promise bids fair yet to be practically fulfilled. Now the point which I ask you to notice is, the play of springs, waters, and inland lakes in them. They are water and insular legends. Their delicacy, their purity, their freshness, their promise, their sense of mystery and of fate, their sense, too, of goodness, of trust, and of love, are water born. They are genuine idyls. But they are insular, they are of springs, streams, and inland lakes. These begot those. From the waters, that is to say, came the

One Type of Nature Teaching.   193

thoughts, the ideals, the aspirations. The whole intellectual and moral fabric, so true to our history, and so prophetic of its issue, is inseparably connected with the power of water over the imagination.

But, as you may consider this too vague and general, I ask you to think of a phenomenon of our own century. Just at its dawn two young men, warm friends, took a journey together into the region of the English Lakes, then little frequented, — and now, by the bye, about to be utilized for the supply of water for the great city of Manchester, perhaps seventy-five miles away. The young men were more than charmed, they were fascinated, by the seclusion of those vales, by the beauty of the wild glens, by the fantastic shapes of the mountains (themselves water-carved), by the humidity of the region which the perfect drainage of the soil hindered nevertheless from being wet, by the play of cloud, mist, and sunlight, but especially by the lakes themselves, and particularly by Grasmere and Rydal Water. One of the young men, by far the greater genius of the two, was enamoured instantly, and kindled the slower susceptibilities of the other. The former of these young men was Samuel Taylor Coleridge. The latter was William Wordsworth. Within a year Wordsworth settled by Grasmere, and in its neighborhood he spent a long life. Coleridge settled by Derwentwater, not far away, but after some years removed to London. It would be easily possible to show that the lives of both these men were definitely affected by the then wild lakes; that the lakes entered into their thinking and their theories; that, in the case of Coleridge, his power over English and American thought in the first half of this century — a power so great that it can hardly be estimated — was largely contributed to by the lakes; and that, as for Wordsworth, who lived by Grasmere and Rydal all his life, and now lies in Grasmere churchyard, and who marks a new epoch in English poetry, the lakes were as the water of life to him. Of Southey, De Quincey, and Scott (whose own lakes were, however, those of the Scottish Highlands), of Wilson, and of Thomas Arnold, much might be said in the same direction. There was never really any "Lake School," except in fancy, but there was a mighty, deathless lake *life*, whose power in English literature and in Anglo-Saxon living will not soon die. And here was done for a few rare minds by these inland lakes and streams, visibly, palpably, and in a way vastly affecting our age, what less palpably, but not less really, was done by the operation of the same causes, through the Arthurian legends, for our Anglo-Saxon people during many centuries.

The reader will observe that the two illustrations are drawn from within the ancient northern glacial belt. It would have been interesting to draw a third from within the same belt on our side of the Atlantic. What Lake Walden and other New England lakes similarly formed, and their associated streams, did for Thoreau, Emerson, and Hawthorne, there is no estimating. Indeed, perhaps Hawthorne is never so much at home in any of his foreign writing as in his English Lake Notes. The waters of the old ice lands, having their own peculiar setting and character, need to be studied in relation to the history of the imagination, and of national spirit, by some one expert both in glacial action, and in literature and folk-lore. Were all the facts known, it would probably appear that the lakes and streams of this belt, presenting as they do a singular combination of thought-impressing elements, have, from the times when man began to think, over and over again induced such personal experiences as the Arthurian legends seem to imply, as the Coleridge-Wordsworthian lakes passion has put into biography, and as Thoreau, the New England solitary, lived out. There seem to have been analogous experiences among our [American] aborigines. It is doubtful if Scandinavian literature can be explained without them.

Appendix A.

The Tell legends spring ashore, as it were, from the Lake of the Four Forest Cantons. How well the ice wrought! How much mightier than Merlin's is the water's enchantment in the old ice lands!

APPENDIX B.

OMITTED PART OF DISCOURSE VI.

NOTE.

"Ye cannot bear them now," said Christ of "many things" he wished to utter, and refrained himself. He is doing so still. And, friend, he is doing so by you and me. This should humble us. It should also give us quick insight and tact what to say to others. For one man's noonday is another's midnight; one man's holiest truth of God, another's heresy or blasphemy. "He hath spoken blasphemy," they said of him, the blameless, to whom belonged perfect vision. Here is one range in which ministers need Christliness. What to say, what not to say, and how to express the message given them, only Christ can teach.

When we had come to the last discourse of this series, I could not go right on, but must pause. The substance of what I said in the pause, follows. It is not included in the discourse as printed, because matter more pertinent to the close of the discussion had a right to be substituted for it there. (See note, p. 161.) It appears here for the same reason that caused it to be spoken, namely, to help any persons who, having come thus far, may need its help. God bless them, every one!

OMITTED PART OF DISCOURSE VI.[1]

THERE is in this age, as in every thinking age, a movement, or progress, of religious thought. This is not a movement of any man, or of any institution, or of any sect or denomination, or of any great division of the Church, such as Presbyterian or Anglican or Lutheran, or such as Protestant or Catholic or Greek, or, indeed, of any yet wider division among men, like that between

---

[1] SYNOPSIS. — There is in this age a movement, or progress, of religious thought. — This not of a man, or institution, or section of the Church, or of the Church itself, exclusively, but of the world. — Multiform, doubtless in error in part, but God-inspired and Godward-moving. — Illustrated by the analogy of the literary movement of the past century within the languages of Europe. — Able to be perceived by us contemporaneously. — Profitable for preaching. — Our Saviour's desire that men should note the signs of the times. — His Spirit to guide into all the truth. — This, properly, the temper of Protestantism, and particularly of Congregationalism. — The preacher had been understood hardly rightly by some, conscientiously, however. — Why he had spoken, with what shrinking, and in what attitude toward the subject. — A personal *Credo*. — Short summary of these discourses. — Christ the centre of the present movement, or progress, — (1) For, etc. [as on page 160].

Christians and those who are Theists merely, or like that between the men of faith and the men of unfaith. It is a movement, rather, of our whole race, in the realm of the religious faculty. It affects different individuals, different classes of men, different divisions of the religious world, variously, according to their characteristics and points of view, but it is one movement, in different parts and in different manifestations.

I hope I make my meaning clear. I am not speaking now of particular religious beliefs. I am speaking of the religious heart of men. This heart is moving. God is touching it. Sometimes it is moving under forms of error, feeling after God. Sometimes it is moving under simple, clear thoughts of God, in holy men as it were seeing him. But it is one movement. And that Infinite Being who lives and moves in all things, lives and moves in it.

Perhaps I can illustrate what I mean from an altogether different subject, namely, literature. We have long known that there was a distinct movement in English literature, beginning late in the last century, blossoming forth early in this, and unfolding with the century. Now those who have given themselves to the comparative study of the literature of the same period in other languages on the Continent of Europe, have discovered, and are gradually tracing out, a corresponding movement in the literature of those languages. The languages were different; the races were different; the points of view were different. But the movement was one, and marked by almost identically the same impulses. This has been specially impressed upon me by a conversation lately had on the subject with a gentleman of high attainments who is making this comparative study his specialty, and who, I hope, will by and by write on it.

Consider, I pray you, what an impressive thing this is, — to know that, while our English literature was taking a new form and bent, almost unwittingly the literature of the Continental languages was taking, intrinsically, a corresponding form and bent. What does such a fact say to us? Does it not say that the men speaking the different languages of Europe, having been for ages under the same general tutelage of civic struggle and of Christian influence, were responding under one and the same guidance of God, to the touch of his breath and mind, and through representative writers, each unknown to the others at the start, were breaking forth into new and higher literary expression? I cannot look at it in any other way. And this circumstance I regard as yet another evidence that the God and Father of us all has not left the world alone, either in religious or in secular matters, but is moving in it, and bending it to his thoughts.

Now, similarly, in the matter of the religious impulse and thought in men, there is a movement, pervasive, world-wide, diverse in form, diverse in expression, often faulty, perchance repeatedly in error, but, in one way or another, feeling its way or thinking its way nearer to God. In ages past, so isolated were men, and so inadequate was their interchange of thought, that such a movement could not be discerned as of wide extent in its time, but was so revealed later to the student of the history of the respective times. But to-day, so near is the world, in its parts, brought to itself as a whole, by steam, electricity, and the printing-press, that we can see on its many sides this movement going on, and, contemporaneously, can watch it.

It has accordingly seemed to me that this impressive thing, the movement of religious thought at the present day, discernible by us contemporaneously, and of as much vaster moment than any movement of literature as religion itself is of vaster moment than literature, would be a profitable subject for our meditation these closing Sunday nights of the year, so far as absence of other Sunday-night appointments left us the evenings free for such meditation. We were to climb, so to speak, into a lofty lookout, and gaze over wide extending land and sea, to observe how the thoughts of men were moving, and how freshly they were thinking of God.

Our Saviour criticised the children of light for not being wise enough in their generation. He indicated that it might be a mark of hypocrisy to have insight about such signs in the outer world as those of the weather, but not to be able to discern the signs of the times. By this, I suppose he meant that the persons addressed, being discerning enough to detect the indications of the face of nature, but wilfully shutting their eyes against the new spiritual light which was breaking upon the world in their time, were not candid; and that, therefore, since they professed to be holy men, they were, in so far, untrue to their profession, or, in other words, hypocritical. And if ever I, for one, find myself unwilling with open eyes to behold the light on religious matters which God is bringing to our time, I shall fear that it is from some timidity or prejudice or self-interest in me; and that thus, professing to be a child of God, I am to this degree hypocritical in it, that I will not let God teach me, his child, the lessons he is trying to teach me.

Our Saviour also affirmed that he had many things to say which men could not then bear, and promised the Spirit of Truth to guide men into all the truth. The same has been the characteristic attitude of Protestantism, — not to fear the truth, but to seek it and be ready for it. The same, particularly, has been the temper of our Congregationalism, Robinson urging the departing Pilgrims to expect fresh light to break from the Bible, and — as an early New England writer reports — deploring the tendency of the Reformation to stick where Luther or Calvin or Knox stopped, instead of, in their spirit, going on into the whole truth as God should continue to make it clear.

I would not say an unkind word of any one, nor judge any one. I would only criticise myself, and judge myself, and I do that severely. But I am at a loss to see how I could have been understood in some instances quite as I have, in the matter of these discourses, — I doubt not conscientiously, and from true motives, so that I entertain for any so understanding me not only respect, but a tender and sincere love. Such are, indeed, among the truest people that I know.

In this spirit of respect and love let us look at the matter for a moment. And, first, speaking generally, think you, dear friends, it is a right thing, or not a right thing, for a Christian preacher to attempt to describe a general age movement of religious thought in this the most wonderful period since Christ left the world?

And, next, speaking personally, do you think that I, who love you, could lightly give you one troubled or anxious moment? I trust what you know of me will lead you to believe otherwise. The fact is,— I may as well confess it,— that when the question arose in my own soul whether I should attempt to do this or not,— and I consulted on the subject with no human being,— I shrank from it almost with trembling. Having put the title of the sermons in the printer's hands for announcement, I came pretty near resolving to draw my pen through the proof, and to have the type distributed before it went to press. And I only refrained from doing so under a solemn conviction of the duty of speaking to my people, and to any who cared to come and hear, of this movement of religious thought in our time,— not as indorsing it in all respects, for in some respects I could not indorse it, but as describing and characterizing it for our information and help; and under a solemn conviction, likewise, that not to speak would be to fail to act the part of the householder spoken of by our Lord, who "bringeth forth out of his treasure things new and old."

And this was all that I was doing. I was not expressing, except where I indicated it, my own opinions, or those of any other man, or of any set of men, or of any institution, or of any wing of thought; but I was characterizing a movement, a trend and march of current history, of which, in one form or another, whether we will or not, we are all a part. And I expressly stated that this movement might err. We are liable to err in everything, particularly in everything new or untried; and I said that it was one of the perils of our time that its newer religious thought might stray in this or that particular.[1]

But what, then, are we to do? Are we to shut our eyes? Are we to stop thinking? When the age is thinking, are we to refuse to consider its thoughts, and learn from them? I cannot do so. Nor can I, as a Christian preacher, think it right to do so by my people. Especially I cannot when I see our Lord, who, had he remained quiet on certain subjects, might have received a wide popular following, refusing to do so, but truly speaking his thought, though death in consequence was certain; and when I see Saint Paul, all through the Acts, while conciliatory and charitable, bearing witness to unpopular truth, and suffering for it. I must follow in our Lord's steps and in Saint Paul's in like exigencies, should they arise.

It has seemed to me right, in this discourse, — which, in closing the series, is partly of the nature of recapitulation, — that I should allude, lovingly,

---

[1] See, for example, p. 109.

to this matter. I again testify to the conscientiousness and true motive, as I trust, of any dissent, and to my love for those who may be in such a case. I can well understand that approach to truth which is theirs, and which seems to compel dissent. And I ask you who, in such numbers, have followed the discourses with eager interest, to have for any such the same respect, love, and sense of point of view. For if any of us have larger light, the proof of the true heart in that light will be love, and love's power to appreciate and understand those who have not the same light.

I ought to add that, while I have not been expounding my opinions, but describing a movement, it is true, nevertheless, that my heart joys and sings with the movement. Not able to agree with it in every particular, I believe its trend to be in the right direction, and it stirs and thrills my whole being. But, lest any misunderstand, I give, what will perhaps be reassuring, this my personal Credo: —

I believe in the living God, Father, Son, and Holy Spirit, one and yet three: the Son and the Spirit with the Father very God: the Son eternally begotten: no man saved except through the Son: no man saved except born into a new life through the Spirit: the Bible, rightly interpreted, the one transcendent literature, pointing us to God, authoritative over life: sin awful, its consequences terrible, its punishment inevitable, perhaps without end: man deathless, to be clothed upon with a spiritual body, hardly so much to be judged as forever being judged by holy, and yet pitying and helping, God, and forever going, under such a God, to his own place: and eye not having seen nor ear heard nor heart of man conceived the things prepared, of good for the true and of evil for the false, in the larger life. Amen.

I should need to say much more, fully to round out what I have put into so few words; and my use of these words might, in turn, easily be misunderstood: but so I believe, sincerely, and not handling the words in any other than their obvious sense. And, so believing, I do not belong under certain denominational names which have been at one time or another spoken of as if they might be mine. I must, however, confess this, that I respect those denominations, love every true soul in them, wish I might go out in outward as well as in spiritual fellowship to them, and believe that they, though I must dissent from them in certain particulars, are, nevertheless, true parts of Christ's Church, are bearing witness to aspects of truth which we are prone to overlook, and are only disfellowshipped by us through what, in the broad light of eternity, will be looked back to as a denying of the very spirit of our Lord, — done, however, through our having honestly mistaken what that spirit was.

I now turn to our subject proper, namely, Christ the centre of the newer religious thinking. But even here, I must delay for a brief recapitulation.

In the first, then, of these discourses I showed that, as there has been in the past, so there is now, a movement of religious thought, — not your movement, or mine, or that of any set of men, or division or denomination of Christendom, but a movement, — and I indicated some of its characteristics.

In the second and third of these discourses I asked you to think of the mighty spring, or motive, underlying this movement. I pointed out how, both in its nature, and as regards the men in it, it is impelled by hunger after God and passion for men; and, also, how this hunger and passion are leading to the re-study — not necessarily the rejection, but the re-study — and more adequate interpretation of some Christian doctrines and practices, with the consequent overthrow of certain idols of the mind in these directions.

In the fourth and fifth discourses I asked you to think of the material, or data, out of which, inductively, this movement is going forward into larger and, as I believe it will ultimately prove, juster and more adequate conceptions of religious truth. I pointed out how it studies two books: the unwritten book, consisting of nature, history, and life, or, in one word, the world; and the written book, the Bible. I pointed out how it seeks to let each book throw light on the other, and help interpret the other; but that it has an undiminished reverence for, and submission to the Bible, rightly understood and interpreted.

It is to this point, then, that we now come in closing; namely, to note that, etc. [as on page 171].

APPENDIX C.

SOME PLAIN QUESTIONING.

NOTE.

There are aspects of discussion which are incapable of systematic treatment. They are matters of point of view, of antagonistic or sympathetic approach, of objections or confirmatory considerations suggested by the mind, etc. They require personal conference, question and answer, and downright, thorough talk. Three supposed persons are accordingly suffered to do some of this hereinafter. One should not forget the dear resurrection dialogue. The voice even of angels suffices not. The questioning mind insists on feeling its own way toward the light. And so it is written:—

I.

They [two angels] say unto her, Woman, why weepest thou?

She saith unto them, Because they have taken away my Lord, and I know not where they have laid him.

II.

She turned herself back, and beholdeth Jesus standing, and knew not that it was Jesus.

Jesus saith unto her, Woman, why weepest thou? whom seekest thou?

She, supposing him to be the gardener, saith unto him, Sir, if thou hast borne him hence, tell me where thou hast laid him, and I will take him away.

Jesus saith unto her, MARY!

She turneth herself, and saith unto him, MASTER!

SOME PLAIN QUESTIONING.

I.

UNDER this "newer religious thinking," which, you say, is not yours, — though I should consider it a tolerably faithful reflection of your ideas, — but which is, the rather, of the time, and, indeed, of all of us, — a statement from which I beg to dissent, — what becomes of the religion of the lowly Jesus?

B. It seems to me, friend, that the religion of Jesus is for the first time beginning to get adequate expression in this thinking.

A. What! in such a worldly time as this? This is not such a time as Edward Payson's, or as Jonathan Edwards's, or as that of the Reformers, to go no farther back.

B. I should hope it might in some ways improve upon those times.

A. But I mean in spirit. We do not pray as much, nor fast as much, nor do we eschew the world as they did.

B. Nor, let me add, as John the Baptist did. "He that is but little in the Kingdom of heaven is greater than he." "The Son of man came eating and drinking."

A. But tell me, if you please, how the religion of the lowly Jesus is, as you have just said, "for the first time beginning to get adequate expression in this thinking."

B. In the matter of God.

A. How?

B. Jesus was in a living touch with his Father. He did not get it roundabout through Moses or Isaiah, but in direct consciousness. So getting it, he swept aside various traditional thoughts of God, to the scandal of many. The newer thinking is in an analogous temper. It, as it were, sees God, and hates the idols which have usurped his place.

A. I call that very irreverent, to say the least. "No man hath seen God at any time." Besides, how can this human thinking, or any other, be likened to the thinking of the omniscient Jesus?

B. "The pure in heart . . . shall see God."

A. In heaven, it means.

B. Yes, and also, in beginnings at least, on earth. We are bidden, moreover, to have the mind in us "which was also in Christ Jesus," and does not that mean that human thinking may — nay, should — be like that of Jesus? He, by the way, has told us that, at least in one particular, he is not omniscient.

A. Well, go on.

B. In this thinking, also, the passion of Jesus for men is waking up.

A. I don't call these university extensions, these boys' clubs, etc., the passion of Jesus for men. He was seeking to save their immortal souls.

B. Did he ever use the expression "immortal soul"? In his personal handling of men did he ordinarily thrust forward that idea? Was he not feeding them, telling them where to cast the net, and becoming the friend of publicans and sinners?

A. Go on.

B. In this thinking, too, to a degree never equalled before, we are getting the approach of Jesus to nature. He was in the most perfect intimacy and harmony with it, no naturalist or poet so much so.[1] In this spirit the newer thinking

---

[1] With the Saviour, let us not forget, it was all vision. He had the second sight. The hen brooding her chickens; the sparrow fallen by the hedgerow; the woman making bread; the mason slowly raising the four walls of a house on rock or on sand; the lily tossing on its stem; the azure or murky sky; the sower going forth to sow; the fishers drawing their nets; the merchantmen passing up and down along the Galilean caravan route; the self-mastered centurions, under authority, and therefore keeping a peace and winning a love among a turbulent population, which proconsul, king, and emperor alike were unable to win; the new Roman coinage finding its beneficent way into Palestine; priest, Levite, and wretched Samaritan; phylacteried and admired Pharisee, and native-born farmer of taxes for the foreigner, universally hated; the wind blowing where it listed; the fig tree

approaches nature, history, and life,—that is to say, the world, or nature in its larger sense.

A. "The approach of Jesus to nature"? He lived above nature, and only used an occasional illustration from it, and—

B. More than "occasional," friend.

A. That does not make any difference. His only use for nature was to illustrate spiritual truth by it.

B. Did he not say that his Father, with whom he was one, fed the birds, and so clothed the grass of the field? Was not a divine intimacy with nature implied?

A. We can't stop to dispute every point. I was about to say that he only used an occasional illustration from nature, and that his strong hold was with Scripture.

B. And there, again, we have, in the newer thinking, an approach to the spirit and meaning of Scripture such as has not been had since Christ. It is for the real life of the Bible, for its very heart, that the newer thinking seeks. The Saviour was

putting forth her leaves; the eagles gathering themselves together, both zoölogical and Roman; Herod's marble wonder, not yet builded after forty and six years,—all, everything, spoke to him, and through him to men. "Never man so spake," they freely said. 'T was because he saw so much. Out of the abundance of the heart the mouth spake.—"*Primary Qualifications for the Ministry,*" *in* "*Andover Review,*" *May-June,* 1893.

doing that. Because he was doing it, his countrymen thought him destroying law and prophets; just as many good people think now regarding some of the most thorough and devout Bible students. And as it is the real life of the Bible, its very heart, that the newer thinking seeks, so, as never before since Christ, it is finding it. Compare, for example, George Adam Smith's Isaiah with even so modern and strong a work as Alexander's on that book.

A. "George Adam Smith's Isaiah"? It is all politics!

B. Which are God in the world. You thought so when the Emancipation Proclamation went into effect.

A. But politics when Lincoln freed the slave and politics now are two very different things.

B. God not in them now?

A. I should sooner call it the Devil in them. But I will ask you one question. What you have said may be all very well in theory, — though, to be frank, I don't believe one syllable of your theory; it seems to me a mere playing with words,— but what becomes of the Bible on such a view of it?

B. Precisely what became of it before. It speaks to life just as then; only its meaning is greatly deepened, because its spirit more than its letter speaks now.

A. But who is to determine what its spirit is? Before these new theories came along, we had a plain "Thus saith the Lord" about everything.

B. Yes, "Thus saith the Lord, Send back the fugitive slaves as Saint Paul sent back Onesimus."

A. I deny that. The pro-slavery men never took the spirit of the Bible. That little epistle to Philemon, only twenty-five verses of it in all, a mere note going back with the man's slave, they made more of than of all the rest of the Bible put together. For my part, when I used to hear the sermons from it, I often wished that Paul had never written it, or Onesimus had lost it, or Philemon's baby had thrown it into the fire.

B. That is the very point. There are other passages, here and there in the Bible, which many a devout soul has wished had never been written, or had been lost, because they have been so misused.

A. Hold! I was only talking about Philemon.

B. But I was talking about some other passages.

A. Then I count what you say heterodox.

B. It is not the first time I have heard that. Let us go back. The anti-slavery people insisted on the spirit of the Bible, and their opponents on its letter; and the latter asked, in effect, precisely the question which you were asking a moment ago, "Who is to determine what its spirit is?"

Ah! my friend, only the living Spirit of God, in the living spirits of men, can determine what the spirit of the Bible is.

A. You mean that nothing is stable?

B. Matters are stable in one sense. They are working ever toward the truth. But nothing is stable in another sense, if it be alive. Growth, continual advance, as you grew from a boy to a man, and as slave days advanced into days of freedom, — this is the order of life.

A. But we have those things now.

B. And would you leave no future for you, and me, and our race?

A. A future in heaven.

B. But what shall we do there, with growth at an end?

A. We shall not get there, if nothing is stable here. I want everything exact, fixed, and mandatory.

B. The craving for that — the craving, that is to say, for outward authority — has taken many a good man to Rome.

A. I am not that kind of a person. I take my stand with the Reformers, and demand a "Thus saith the Lord" for everything.

B. Not apprehending what the spirit of the Reformers was, my friend. But let us see. Was not that what your son desired last night? Perplexed on a certain question, did he not ask you to tell him just what to do? But you did not tell him. You were too sensible to do so. You said, "My son, you have arrived at years of discretion, and while I will give you any light on this matter which I can, you must be a man now, and decide your own questions." You did not give him, in other words, for reasons which seemed to you wise, what he wanted, namely, a "Thus saith my father."

A. But that was only on a business matter. To learn business, a man must use his own head, not some other person's. But, for the infinite concerns of the immortal soul, a "Thus saith the Lord" is needed; not a "Thus saith President Harper, or Professor Briggs, or these new departure preachers that are getting into the pulpits nowadays."

B. Do you mean to say that, in order to train your son for business life, finer methods are needed than to train him and you and me for our being about our Father's business forever?

A. That is how you play with words. There is no logic in theology nowadays, no major premise, minor premise, nor conclusion. I have been wasting your time and mine, too, in so long a talk. Here comes Mr. C. He is one of your kind. I don't mean you any harm, remember. Good-day.

B. I had rather you would harm me than harm my influence. But God will take care of that. Good-day, and may he be with and bless you!

II.

C. Good-morning.

B. Good-morning.

C. I am so glad I have found you. I take the train to-night for my little mission among the mountains. We shall not have a chance to do church work together again, perhaps ever, nor shall we meet for a long time. I want to ask you some questions. Put the answers in pat.

B. I have not much wisdom. Let us have the questions. I will do the best I can with them.

C. Is there, to begin with, any truth in the sneering remark that the newer religious thinking "is a theology without a theologian"?

B. We have the same state of things in that matter which always ensues when general work, which has probably inclined to *a priori*, yields place to induction, with detailed work. The latter sets everybody a task. There are fifty or five hundred scientists, or theologians, where there used to be five. They subdivide the subject. Each toils in his own field. There is, thus, not the chance for individual prominence which there once was.

The popular imagination, therefore, is not so much appealed to, and the remark you quote is readily caught up. "Make us a king to judge us," the popular imagination is always demanding, no longer of Samuel, but of theology. But the remark is very superficial. It would imply, in principle, that natural history in America is going backward because no man among us has succeeded to the precise eminence of Agassiz. Agassiz, on the contrary, strove to pass the blessing on to thousands. This was the meaning of his summer schools. It is inconceivable that he could make such a remark of the newer science, were he still with us, as this about the newer religious thinking.

C. What you say leads to my second question: Is our instruction in theology up to the necessities of the hour?

B. On the whole it is doing well,—in some of our institutions very well. There does not always go with the necessary subdivision of work so much of a unifying spirit as there should. There is lack, sometimes, of a temper, in this respect, like Agassiz's in natural history, or Mark Hopkins's in ethics. Neither has theology proper, as it seems to me, enough broken with the old topical divisions, subdivisions, etc. The Linnæan classification in Botany had its uses, but was obliged to yield to a better. Courage and constructive genius are needed in this respect. All things considered, however, — for we must not forget that we are in a change of outlook almost revolutionary, and that the conditions of work are therefore difficult, — the situation is gratifying, though there are some things yet to be desired.

C. I am glad to hear you say so. Is there not, however, danger that the newer approach to truth will constitute yet another dogmatism?

B. Certainly. In individuals it surely will. Few men have the calibre and heart to remain always teachable and learning. Against this peril in ourselves let us both strive. But I think, under the inductive spirit, dogmatism can never again reign. When I spoke of "constructive genius," I did not mean constructive of dogmatic systems. Their day has passed.

C. Bless God, if it shall prove so! I think I have heard you say that there is an advantage for the Old Testament in the new view of it?

B. A very great advantage. Before, its uses were fragmentary. Certain passages, certain phrases, and here and there a portion of it, were specially comforting or helpful, but, as a whole, particularly in the prophets, it was a sort of *terra incognita*, however well traversed by the reader. Everything in it, on the contrary, now leaps into meaning. The life within it speaks. We see it growing, advancing, struggling in the process, but victorious. Some one has likened this to the difference between knowing the perorations of Burke or Webster, and knowing the men themselves and the national crises through which they passed.

C. That is what I so much like about the new idea of the Bible. God's living Spirit and men's spirits are brought to the front. There is a voice now as truly as to Moses or Isaiah. For this the Bible is finger-board, indicates directions, suggests, stirs the heart. It is an indispensable auxiliary. Breathing with intense life, it is a kind of Marseillaise Hymn to which the soul marches. But it is no longer put forward as if it were itself life. It does not bind thought and truth fast forever. Individual men, the human race, and the heavenly life, are left their chance to expand evermore. The crustacean stage is over.

B. You catch the thought.

C. I am so thankful that you magnify Christ. I have two perplexities there, however. One of them is practical. How can so broad a Christian union as you yearn for come while some whom you would include in it believe Christ to be far less than most who are to be included in it believe him to be?

B. Saint John had that difficulty. It was he

who spoke where we read: "Master, we saw one casting out devils in thy name; and we forbade him, because he followeth not with us. But Jesus said unto him, Forbid him not: for he that is not against you is for you." Our Lord seems also to have had in view and been hospitable toward the two types of mental outlook when he said, "Believe me that I am in the Father, and the Father in me: or else believe me for the very works' sake." There exist necessarily these two types. Their existence should be a perpetual caution to us not to be too certain that we have compassed this great subject. But, in any case, the irrepressible yearning of Christendom in our time to be one is a voice of God, if ever God spoke in the soul of an age.

C. So it seems to me, though there are complexities about the problem. But, again, you speak of the infinite Christ principle, the Lamb slain from the foundation of the world. Is this concept enough?

B. No. No concept is enough. There are as many sides of Christ as there are of this round globe. We must be open and alert for all of them. But this concept is primary. It will last us a good while. The skipper's boy, you remember, having been told to steer the sloop by a certain star, woke him up after a little, saying, "Father, give me another star, I've got past that one." We shall not soon get past this.

C. Indeed we shall not. Do you not think, to touch on another subject, that there is a practical peril about what is called the "larger hope"?

B. Yes. And there was practical peril about the old eschatology. It was the wrecking of many a man's faith. It hardened men. The "larger hope" has, no one should forget, a sense, almost awful, of the evil of sin and of its sure punishment in any event. With this, on the other hand, it couples thoughts of God worthier, as it believes, than those of the other view.

C. I think that a fair way to put it. Only one question more. Does the newer thinking make as good Christians?

B. How good Christians?

C. As good as the old made.

B. How good did the old make?

C. Well, I admit that it did not always make good ones; it made, for instance, Judas, and Cardinal Wolsey, and — well, me.

B. Have you not known Christians holding obvious errors who were shining Christians, nevertheless?

C. Yes.

B. And Christians holding ideal views who, notwithstanding, belied the name of Christ?

C. Yes.

B. While we recognize, then, that a transitional period in thought, like that in which we now are, must affect temporarily some Christian life for the better and some for the worse, shall we not say, nevertheless, that it is not the thinking that makes the Christian, but the following Christ that makes him?

C. That is it.

B. And you and I will do it?

C. God helping us, we will. Good-by.

B. Good-by, and may God bless the little mission among the mountains!

In how many and what uncertain words do men strive to express the simplest truth when that truth is only dawning on themselves and on others! It is like the shrill, disordered jargoning of birds when morning first flushes the east. Presently the whole firmament glows, the sun is up, the mists flee away, jargon is done, and day reigns.

LIST OF PRINCIPAL NOTES.

	PAGE
Concerning these Discourses	13, 161, 198
Had Christ Mental Advance during his Ministry?	15
Mr. Bullard and Dr. Bushnell	17
Professor Tucker's " From Liberty to Unity ".	27
Dr. Sheldon (and see text)	32
Channing, Parker, Emerson, Carlyle	43
" Plain Words on our Lord's Work "	53
Capital and Labor	92
Restoring the Order of Israelitish History	150
Professor Thayer and Dr. Gladden on the Bible	152
Dr. Edgerly (and see text)	166
How Camelot looked as men approached it	170
Disfellowshipping Drs. Hale, Peabody, and Others	178
Death the Enhancing of Phillips Brooks's Influence	180
Heresy of the Antithesis between Nature and God	188
" Ye cannot bear them now "	198
The Resurrection Dialogue	212
With the Saviour it was all vision	215

*I saw a new heaven and a new earth.
I saw no temple therein.
His servants shall serve him.
They shall see his face.
His name shall be in their foreheads.
There shall be no night there.
I John saw these things, and heard them.
Love is of God.
Every one that loveth is born of God, and knoweth God.*

SAINT JOHN.

www.ingramcontent.com/pod-product-compliance
Lightning Source LLC
Chambersburg PA
CBHW020812230426
43666CB00007B/983